A History of Qatar

Ahmad Rezeq

Table of Contents

- **Introduction**

- **Chapter 1** The Dawn of Settlement: Qatar's Prehistoric Era

- **Chapter 2** From Kassites to Sasanians: Early Empires and the Qatar Peninsula

- **Chapter 3** The Arrival of Islam and the Umayyad Era

- **Chapter 4** The Abbasid Caliphate and the Rise of Local Powers

- **Chapter 5** The Age of Pearling and Trade: Qatar in the Medieval World

- **Chapter 6** The Portuguese and Ottoman Sway: A Contest for the Gulf

- **Chapter 7** The Rise of the Al Thani: The Foundation of Modern Qatar

- **Chapter 8** Sheikh Jassim bin Mohammed Al Thani: Unifier and Founder

- **Chapter 9** The Anglo-Qatari Treaty of 1916: A New Era of Protection

- **Chapter 10** The Great Depression and the Decline of the Pearl Industry

- **Chapter 11** The Dawn of the Oil Age: The First Concessions and Discoveries

- **Chapter 12** Post-War Boom: The Transformation of Qatari Society

- **Chapter 13** The Road to Independence: The 1960s and British Withdrawal

- **Chapter 14** Statehood and the Early Years of Independence: 1971-1980

- **Chapter 15** Navigating Regional Politics: The Iran-Iraq War and the GCC

- **Chapter 16** The North Field Discovery: The Gas Revolution Begins

- **Chapter 17** The 1995 Palace Coup and the Rise of Sheikh Hamad bin Khalifa Al Thani

- **Chapter 18** Al Jazeera and the New Public Diplomacy: Qatar on the World Stage

- **Chapter 19** Economic Diversification and the Qatar National Vision 2030

- **Chapter 20** Education City and the Knowledge Economy

- **Chapter 21** Hosting the World: The 2006 Asian Games and the Bid for the World Cup

- **Chapter 22** The Arab Spring and Qatar's Foreign Policy

- **Chapter 23** The 2017 Diplomatic Crisis: Blockade and Resilience

- **Chapter 24** The FIFA World Cup 2022: Triumph and Controversy

- **Chapter 25** Qatar in the 21st Century: Challenges and Future Prospects

- **Afterword**

Introduction

To gaze upon the skyline of modern Doha is to witness a statement of intent written in steel and glass. Mirrored skyscrapers, sculpted with impossible geometries, sprout from the desert edge, reflecting the turquoise waters of the Persian Gulf. Man-made islands blossom into opulent residential and commercial districts, connected by sprawling highways and a gleaming, driverless metro system. This is a cityscape born of staggering wealth and boundless ambition, a global hub for finance, media, and international sport, famously culminating in the spectacle of the 2022 FIFA World Cup. It is a vision of the future, meticulously planned and lavishly funded, that has materialized in the space of a single generation.

Yet, to understand the story of Qatar is to peel back this glossy veneer of hyper-modernity and discover a narrative far more complex and improbable. Less than a century ago, the very land on which these architectural marvels stand was an impoverished, sparsely populated backwater. Its inhabitants, living in small coastal villages, were subject to the whims of a harsh desert climate and the perilous fortunes of the pearl trade. Life was a precarious cycle of seasonal migration, tribal rivalries, and colonial oversight. The Qatar that existed then is almost unrecognizable from the nation that commands the world's attention today. This book asks a simple, yet profound, question: how did this happen? How did a tiny, arid peninsula, long considered a peripheral territory by regional empires, transform itself into one of the wealthiest and most influential nations, per capita, on Earth?

The answer is a multifaceted story of geography, fortune, and human endeavor. It is a history shaped by the very land itself—a thumb-like projection of the Arabian Peninsula, approximately 11,586 square kilometers of mostly flat, rocky desert. For millennia, this unforgiving environment dictated the terms of existence. Human occupation dates back at least 50,000 years, with evidence of Stone Age encampments, but sustained settlement was sparse. Early inhabitants were drawn to the coast, where the sea offered a livelihood that the arid interior could not. The peninsula was never the heart of an empire, but rather a crossroads and a resource, influenced by the great civilizations of Mesopotamia and Persia, and later falling within the orbit of the Dilmun maritime trading network. It was a land people passed through, a coast to be harvested for its rich pearl banks, but rarely a destination in its own right.

Over the centuries, the strategic waters of the Gulf brought the contest for influence to Qatar's shores. The peninsula felt the sway of early Islamic caliphates, becoming a center for the pearl trade by the 8th century during the Abbasid era. Later, the ambitions of European powers manifested in the region, with the Portuguese making their presence felt in the 16th century, followed by a prolonged period of rivalry with the Ottoman Empire. For much of its history, Qatar was not a distinct political entity but a territory contested by its more powerful neighbors, including the rulers of Bahrain and the rising powers of the Arabian interior. This long experience of being a pawn in a larger game would instill in its future leaders a deep-seated desire for sovereignty and self-determination.

Central to this story is the rise of a single family: the Al Thani. Their modern history begins in the 18th century, as they and other tribes consolidated their presence on the peninsula. In a landscape defined by shifting tribal allegiances and external pressures from the Ottomans and the British, the Al Thani navigated a treacherous path. Through shrewd diplomacy, political acumen, and the forging of a crucial treaty with Great Britain in 1868 that recognized Qatar's separate status from Bahrain, Sheikh Mohammed bin Thani laid the foundation for a modern state. His son, Sheikh Jassim bin Mohammed Al Thani, is revered as the true founder, a unifier who defended the peninsula against both Ottoman and regional threats, forging a nascent sense of national identity in the crucible of conflict.

For generations, the economic lifeblood of this emerging statelet was the pearl. The pearling industry shaped the culture, social structure, and rhythms of daily life. Each summer, the majority of the male population would set sail on dhows for months of grueling and dangerous work, diving into the depths of the Gulf. The fortunes of the entire community rested on the success of the annual harvest. Then, in the 1920s and 1930s, this centuries-old way of life collapsed with breathtaking speed. The global economic depression, combined with the Japanese invention of the cultured pearl, rendered Qatar's primary export virtually worthless overnight. The peninsula plunged into a period of extreme poverty and hardship, with its population dwindling as families sought survival elsewhere.

It was at this nadir of its fortunes that Qatar's destiny was irrevocably altered. In 1939, oil was discovered at Dukhan on the western coast. Though the outbreak of World War II delayed commercial exploitation, the post-war era unleashed a torrent of wealth that was previously unimaginable. The first oil exports in 1949 marked the beginning of a profound transformation, not just of the economy, but of society itself. Oil revenues funded the construction of schools, hospitals, roads, and the basic infrastructure of a modern state, pulling the country out of the ashes of the pearling industry's collapse.

This newfound wealth coincided with a changing geopolitical landscape. In 1968, Great Britain announced its intention to withdraw its military and political presence from the Gulf. After brief negotiations to form a federation with neighboring emirates, Qatar chose the path of full independence, which it formally declared on September 3, 1971. The early decades of statehood were focused on nation-building, creating government institutions, and managing the complexities of oil wealth under the leadership of the Al Thani rulers. Yet, a second, even more significant, economic revolution was on the horizon.

The discovery and subsequent development of the North Field—the world's largest non-associated natural gas field—would catapult Qatar into a different league entirely. The visionary, and colossally expensive, decision to pioneer the liquefied natural gas (LNG) industry in the 1990s secured the nation's prosperity for generations to come. This immense gas wealth provided the financial firepower for Qatar to pursue a new and audacious ambition: to carve out a significant role for itself on the global stage.

This ambition was driven forward by the 1995 accession of Sheikh Hamad bin Khalifa Al Thani, who envisioned a future for Qatar that transcended its identity as a hydrocarbon exporter. His reign unleashed a wave of transformative initiatives. The founding of the Al Jazeera satellite news network in 1996 gave Qatar a powerful and often controversial voice across the Arab world and beyond. The establishment of Education City, a sprawling campus hosting branches of elite international universities, signaled a commitment to building a knowledge-based economy.

Simultaneously, Qatar pursued a foreign policy of active and assertive diplomacy. Leveraging its economic clout and reputation as a neutral mediator, it sought to punch far above its weight in regional and international affairs. This independent streak, however, often put it at odds with its larger neighbors, most notably Saudi Arabia. Qatar's support for various movements during the Arab Spring and its complex relationship with regional powers ultimately led to a severe diplomatic crisis in 2017, when a coalition of nations imposed a sudden and comprehensive blockade. This moment of crisis became a defining test of Qatar's resilience and its ability to sustain its hard-won independence.

This book charts this extraordinary journey, from its prehistoric origins to its status as a 21st-century global player. It is a chronological exploration of the forces that have shaped this land and its people: the ancient rhythms of desert and sea, the currents of trade and empire, the unifying leadership of a ruling dynasty, the cataclysmic collapse of one economy and the explosive birth of another, and the deliberate and strategic deployment of immense wealth to secure a place in the modern world. It is the story of a nation's improbable rise, a testament to how history can be transformed in the blink of an eye by a combination of geological luck and bold, strategic vision. The chapters that follow will delve into the details of this remarkable transformation, beginning, as all stories must, at the very beginning—in the dawn of human settlement on the Qatar peninsula.

CHAPTER ONE: The Dawn of Settlement: Qatar's Prehistoric Era

To picture the Qatar Peninsula in the depths of prehistory is to conjure a world almost alien to the one we know today. The familiar palette of sun-bleached sand and rock must be replaced with the greens of savanna and steppe, a landscape sustained by a climate far wetter and more hospitable than the present. This was a "Green Arabia," a land of seasonal lakes and meandering river channels, part of a vast, temperate corridor that pulsed with life, attracting both animal herds and the earliest humans who hunted them. It is in this radically different environment that the story of Qatar begins, a story pieced together not from written chronicles, but from the faintest of traces left upon the land: a chipped flint tool, a shard of painted pottery, a mound of discarded shells.

The very first Qataris were ephemeral figures, leaving almost no mark on the landscape. Human occupation of the peninsula stretches back tens of thousands of years, into the mists of the Paleolithic, or Old Stone Age. Archaeological work, pioneered by Danish teams in the 1950s and 60s, uncovered scores of sites littered with primitive stone implements. Along the coastlines and interior ridges, these early hunter-gatherers left behind thousands of flint tools—scrapers, cutters, and arrowheads—which speak to a life of constant movement. These were small, nomadic bands, whose existence was dictated by the migration of game and the availability of fresh water. They built no permanent structures, their shelters likely being temporary encampments of animal hide or brush that have long since vanished. The artifacts they left are the sole testament to their presence, whispers of a time when the peninsula was a hunter's paradise, a verdant frontier for early modern humans making their way out of Africa and across the Arabian landmass.

As millennia passed, the great ice sheets that had locked up much of the world's water retreated, and the global climate began to shift. Around 8,000 years ago, the flooding of the Persian Gulf basin slowed, and the Qatari peninsula, as we know it, took its final shape. This geological event coincided with the dawn of a new era: the Neolithic, or New Stone Age. The climate, while beginning a slow march toward greater aridity, was still significantly wetter than it is today, supporting a wider range of wildlife and vegetation. For the people of Qatar, this new stability, combined with the formation of a long and resource-rich coastline, prompted a fundamental change in lifestyle. The relentless roaming of the Paleolithic gave way to a more settled, though still semi-nomadic, existence centered on the sea.

It is during this Neolithic period that the first true settlements emerge in the archaeological record. Sites clustered along the coast, such as Al Da'asa, Shagra, Wadi Debayan, and Ras Abrouq, provide the most compelling evidence of these early communities. Danish and British-led excavations at Al Da'asa, on the western coast, revealed a site that was likely a seasonal encampment for a fishing, hunting, and gathering group. The most telling discoveries were nearly sixty fire pits, or hearths, suggesting that a group of families returned to this spot repeatedly. These were not just for cooking; the sheer number of hearths hints at a larger purpose, possibly the curing and drying of fish on a significant scale. Scattered among the fire pits were the tools of their trade: flint scrapers, blades, and arrowheads, alongside fragments of stone querns used for grinding. While no complete skeletons of their dwellings remain, the discovery of postholes indicates they lived in tents or simple huts, easily dismantled and moved.

The real surprise of the Neolithic sites, however, was the pottery. Amidst the locally made flint tools, archaeologists unearthed numerous shards of distinctive, painted ceramic ware. This was Ubaid pottery, a product of the advanced civilization that was flourishing hundreds of miles away in Mesopotamia, the land between the Tigris and Euphrates rivers in modern-day Iraq. Originating from southern Mesopotamian cities like Ur and Eridu between 6500 and 3800 BC, the presence of this pottery in Qatar is the first concrete evidence of the peninsula's connection to the wider world. The geometric patterns painted in black or brown on buff-colored clay are unmistakable. Its discovery at multiple sites across the peninsula, from Al Da'asa to Al Khor Island, proves that the people of Qatar were not living in isolation. They were participants in a vast, prehistoric trade network that crisscrossed the Persian Gulf, exchanging local resources—perhaps dried fish, pearls, or hides—for the sophisticated pottery of their powerful northern neighbors.

Life was not solely about subsistence. Discoveries at a Neolithic cemetery in Wadi Al Debaian have offered profound insights into the culture and beliefs of these early coastal dwellers. In 2022, an excavation uncovered a grave dating to 4600 BCE, and with it, the oldest known natural pearl bead ever found in Qatar. This single, tiny object speaks volumes. It is the earliest direct evidence of pearling, an activity that would one day define the region's entire economy. Its placement in a grave suggests that pearls already held a special, perhaps spiritual or social, significance. The burial itself points to a community with established rituals for honoring their dead, a clear indicator of a developing social structure. The presence of obsidian from Anatolia (modern Turkey) at the same site further underscores the astonishing reach of these Neolithic trade routes.

As the fourth millennium BC drew to a close, a new material began to transform the ancient world: bronze. The Bronze Age (roughly 3200-1200 BCE) was a period of increasing social complexity, technological innovation, and expanding trade. For Qatar, this era was defined by its relationship with the great maritime trading power of the Gulf: the Dilmun civilization. Centered in modern-day Bahrain, Dilmun was the crucial middleman in a trade network that linked the powerhouse civilizations of Mesopotamia with the resource-rich lands of the Indus Valley (in modern Pakistan and India) and Magan (Oman). Though not a central part of the Dilmun state itself, the Qatar peninsula lay firmly within its sphere of influence, acting as a resource and a waystation.

Evidence of the Dilmun connection is found in the form of Barbar pottery, a type of ceramic ware characteristic of the Dilmun heartland, which has been unearthed at sites in Qatar. Excavations have revealed settlements from this period at Lusail and, most remarkably, on Jazirat bin Ghanim, an island in a sheltered bay near the modern city of Al Khor. Here, inhabitants lived in semi-subterranean huts, their floors dug into the earth and topped with low walls, likely covered by roofs of thatch or reeds. They sustained themselves through fishing, herding animals, and, crucially, by harvesting the sea for a commodity that was, in its own way, as precious as gold.

Today, Jazirat bin Ghanim is better known by a more evocative name: Purple Island. It was here, during the second millennium BCE, that a highly specialized and valuable industry flourished under the control of the Kassites, a dynasty that ruled Babylonia in Mesopotamia. Excavations on the island have uncovered a truly staggering sight: a midden containing an estimated three million crushed shells of the *Murex* sea snail. These snails were not a source of food. They were the raw material for one of the ancient world's most coveted luxury goods: Tyrian purple dye. The process of extracting the dye was painstaking. Thousands of snails had to be harvested, their glands removed and processed to produce a tiny amount of a fluid that, when exposed to sunlight, transformed into a brilliant, colorfast purple. The resulting dye was astronomically expensive, its use reserved for the robes of royalty, nobility, and high priests across Mesopotamia and the wider Near East. Purple Island was, in essence, an industrial-scale factory, a seasonal outpost dedicated to producing this marker of ultimate status for a foreign power. The presence of Kassite-era potsherds alongside the shell heaps confirms the connection, painting a vivid picture of Qatari waters being harvested to clothe the kings of Babylon.

Beyond this remarkable dye industry, life in Bronze Age Qatar continued to revolve around the sea. Burial mounds from the period, particularly cairns excavated at Ras Abrouq, have yielded jewelry made from shells and beads of carnelian, a stone not native to Qatar, further evidence of ongoing trade. A single bronze arrowhead found at Al Wusail is a rare but significant find from this period. The economy was a blend of local subsistence and international trade. The people fished and hunted, herded livestock, and dived for pearls, all while contributing to a globalized Bronze Age economy that connected them to distant empires. Their position was peripheral, yet essential, providing unique resources that were valued far beyond their shores.

The vibrant activity of the Bronze Age appears to have faded as the climate of the peninsula took a decisive turn toward the arid conditions that prevail today. The subsequent period, the Iron Age (c. 1200 BCE onwards), is something of a dark age in Qatar's archaeological story. Unlike the preceding eras, there is a distinct lack of evidence for any significant, permanent settlements. This scarcity of findings suggests that the changing environment may have made a settled, coastal lifestyle difficult to sustain. The population likely dwindled, with many returning to a more nomadic existence, following scarce water and grazing lands for their herds.

The most substantial remains from this period are burial sites. In northwestern Qatar, a site containing around fifty stone cairns was excavated, some of which contained iron arrowheads and even an iron sword alongside the skeletons of those interred. These grave goods, dating from between 300 BCE and 300 CE, hint at a society of nomads, warriors, and traders traversing the peninsula. The Greek historian Herodotus, writing in the 5th century BCE, provided the first known written description of the peninsula's inhabitants, whom he referred to as sea-faring Canaanites, suggesting a people still known for their maritime skills. But without the remains of their towns and villages, the picture is incomplete. This period of relative silence, of sparse population and nomadic rhythms, would last for centuries. The peninsula became a marginal land, a place to pass through rather than to settle, awaiting the arrival of the great empires and new faiths that would shape the next chapter of its long and varied history.

CHAPTER TWO: From Kassites to Sasanians: Early Empires and the Qatar Peninsula

The passing of the Bronze Age and the onset of a harsher, drier climate drew a veil over the Qatar Peninsula. For centuries, the archaeological record falls nearly silent, the vibrant coastal industries and far-flung trade connections seemingly fading like a desert mirage. Yet, the peninsula did not vanish. It merely receded into the background, a fringe territory on the periphery of great powers whose ambitions were focused elsewhere. To trace Qatar's story through this long interlude is to look for its faint reflection in the grand chronicles of Mesopotamia and Persia, and to listen for its name being whispered, however rarely, by the geographers of the classical world. The story is no longer one of local settlement, but of the long shadows cast by distant empires.

The Kassite connection to the purple dye factories on Jazirat bin Ghanim, which flourished in the second millennium BCE, was a telling prologue to this new reality. The Kassites were a people of obscure origin, possibly from the Zagros Mountains, who came to rule Babylonia for over four centuries, the longest dynasty in its history. Their interest in Qatar was not one of conquest or colonization, but of pure, targeted resource extraction. The peninsula's coastal waters provided a unique commodity—the *Murex* snail—that produced a dye of immense value, a color reserved for the elite of their powerful Mesopotamian kingdom. Potsherds left amidst the millions of crushed shells are the calling cards of this enterprise, evidence of a relationship where Qatar served as a specialized, seasonal industrial zone for a foreign power, its local inhabitants providing labor or access in exchange for goods.

As the Kassites faded, a succession of powerful empires rose and fell in the Near East, each dominating the vital trade routes of the Persian Gulf. The aggressive Assyrians and their successors, the

Neo-Babylonians, were followed by the vast Achaemenid Persian Empire founded by Cyrus the Great. These empires treated the Gulf as a crucial artery of commerce and a strategic frontier. While direct archaeological evidence of their presence in Qatar is minimal, the peninsula would have been a known, if minor, feature on their maritime maps. It was a coastline to be navigated, a potential source of fresh water for passing ships, and a home to a sparse population of seafarers and nomads.

It is during this era of Persian dominance that Qatar first enters the written record, albeit obliquely. The Greek historian Herodotus, writing in the 5th century BCE, described the inhabitants of the region as "sea-faring Canaanites," a testament to their enduring maritime identity. A few centuries later, two figures from the Greco-Roman world would finally put a name to the place. In the mid-first century CE, the Roman writer Pliny the Elder wrote of the inhabitants of the peninsula, whom he called the *Catharrei*. A century after Pliny, the Alexandrian geographer Claudius Ptolemy produced a remarkably detailed map of the known world, and on it, he labeled the peninsula itself as *Catara*, even referencing a settlement named *Cadara* on its eastern coast. Though their coordinates were approximate and their knowledge based on sailors' reports, these references are monumental. They confirm that this spit of land, so long anonymous in the grand sweep of history, was recognized by the geographers of the classical world as a distinct place with its own name.

The conquests of Alexander the Great in the 4th century BCE ushered in the Hellenistic Age, and control of the Persian heartland passed to his general Seleucus I, founder of the Seleucid Empire. The Seleucids, deeply enmeshed in Greek culture, maintained a strong interest in the Gulf's trade routes, which now connected their Mediterranean-facing empire with the riches of India. They established major trading posts in the Gulf, most notably on the islands of Ikaros (modern Failaka in Kuwait) and Tylos (modern Bahrain). While Qatar was not a major Hellenistic center, it was undeniably part of this interconnected world.

Tangible proof of this connection lay buried in the Qatari soil for more than two millennia. In the mid-20th century, a hoard of exquisite silver coins was unearthed at Murwab. These were Seleucid coins, most likely tetradrachms, depicting the heads of Hellenistic rulers on one side and figures from Greek mythology, such as Herakles or Zeus, on the reverse. The discovery of these coins is a powerful indicator of economic activity. They were not simply curiosities; they were hard currency, used by merchants and sailors plying the Gulf. Their presence suggests that Qatari pearls, dried fish, or other local goods were being traded into the wider Seleucid economy, linking the peninsula's inhabitants to a commercial network that stretched from the Aegean Sea to the Indus Valley.

The decline of the Seleucids saw the rise of two new superpowers: the Parthian Empire based in Persia and the ever-expanding Roman Empire in the west. The Persian Gulf became a zone of strategic importance and commercial rivalry. It was a key segment of the maritime routes that bypassed the overland Silk Road, connecting the Roman world with the markets of the East. The peninsula once again found its place on the map, with Pliny the Elder noting the "Cataraei" as one of the nomadic tribes inhabiting the region. Archaeological finds from this period are scarce, limited mainly to burial cairns in the northwest which have yielded iron arrowheads and even a sword, grave goods of a nomadic or semi-nomadic people.

It was the arrival of the next great Persian dynasty, the Sasanians, in 224 CE that would bring the Qatar Peninsula back into sharper focus. The Sasanian Empire was a highly centralized and powerful state, a true rival to the Romans and their successors, the Byzantines. They viewed the Persian Gulf not just as a trade route, but as a "Sasanian lake," an integral part of their imperial domain. Consequently, they exerted far more direct influence over the region than their predecessors, and the archaeological evidence reflects this. Sasanian-era settlements and artifacts, including distinctive pottery and glassware, have been found at multiple sites in Qatar, such as Mezru'ah and Umm al-Ma'a, suggesting a more settled and integrated presence. The peninsula contributed valuable commodities to the Sasanian economy, most notably its prized pearls and the purple dye that had first attracted the Kassites.

The most profound development of the Sasanian period, however, was not economic but spiritual. Under Sasanian rule, Christianity, which had been spreading eastward from Mesopotamia for centuries, took firm root in the communities along the Gulf coast. The particular branch that flourished here was the Church of the East, often referred to by outsiders as Nestorianism. Persecuted as heretics within the Byzantine Empire, its followers found a degree of safety and tolerance in the lands controlled by the Sasanians. Over time, a vibrant and intellectually sophisticated Christian community emerged across the region.

Syriac texts from the 4th to the 9th centuries refer to this region, encompassing modern Qatar, Bahrain, and the adjacent coastline, as *Beth Qatraye*—literally, "the region of the Qataris." This was not a backwater but an important ecclesiastical and cultural center. It was home to monasteries and bishoprics, and its scholars were renowned. The inhabitants of Beth Qatraye were active in the intellectual life of their time, known for translating religious and scholarly texts between Persian, Syriac, and Arabic. Indeed, one of the most revered saints and mystical writers in the Syriac tradition, Isaac of Nineveh (also known as Isaac the Qatari), was born on the peninsula in the 7th century.

Archaeological discoveries have provided startling confirmation of this written history. The remains of a structure near Al Wakrah, built on limestone bedrock and dating to the early 7th century, are believed to be a church. The layout and associated ceramics bear a strong resemblance to other Nestorian sites in the Gulf. This, and other finds, paint a picture of a settled, pre-Islamic Christian population living in Qatar. They were likely Aramaic and Syriac speakers, deeply involved in the maritime trade, pearling, and the intellectual currents of their age.

Therefore, on the eve of the arrival of Islam, the Qatar Peninsula was far from an empty quarter. It was a complex and diverse land. In the arid interior, nomadic Arab tribes likely continued their pastoralist lifestyle, following traditional beliefs. Along the coasts, however, were established communities that were part of a wider Sasanian political and economic sphere and, crucially, were integrated into the rich Christian culture of the Near East. They were governed indirectly by the Sasanians, probably through their Arab client kings, the Lakhmids of Al-Hira, who acted as intermediaries and patrolled the desert frontiers. This settled, literate, and globally connected society was the stage upon which the next, and most transformative, chapter of Qatar's history was about to unfold.

CHAPTER THREE: The Arrival of Islam and the Umayyad Era

In the early 7th century, the Qatar Peninsula was a land of multiple identities. Along its coasts, settled communities looked eastward across the sea, their lives intertwined with the Sasanian Persian Empire and their spiritual world shaped by the Syriac traditions of the Church of the East. In the arid interior, nomadic Arab tribes roamed, their loyalties and beliefs rooted in the ancient rhythms of the peninsula. This complex society, known to Christian scholars as *Beth Qatraye*, was about to be irrevocably changed by a new force emerging with astonishing speed from the west—the message of Islam.

The catalyst for this transformation arrived not with an army, but in the form of a letter. Around the year 628 CE, the Prophet Muhammad, having consolidated his position in Medina, began a campaign of correspondence, sending envoys to the rulers of the surrounding lands inviting them to embrace Islam. One such envoy, Al-Ala Al-Hadrami, was dispatched to the wider region of historical Bahrain, which at the time encompassed the Qatar Peninsula and the coastline of modern-day eastern Saudi Arabia. The letter was addressed to the local ruler, a man named Mundhir bin Sawa Al-Tamimi, who governed the territory as a client of the Sasanian kings.

The arrival of Al-Ala Al-Hadrami with the Prophet's message presented Mundhir bin Sawa with a momentous choice. He could remain loyal to his weakening Persian overlords, reject the new faith, or embrace the call from Medina. In a decision that would define the future of the region, Mundhir bin Sawa accepted Islam. His conversion was not a solitary act; historical accounts relate that he was joined by most of the Arab tribes under his rule, and even some of the Persian settlers living in the area. This pivotal event brought Qatar and its people into the fold of the nascent Islamic state, marking the beginning of a profound cultural and religious shift.

The transition was not instantaneous. The Christian communities of *Beth Qatraye*, with their established bishoprics and monasteries, did not vanish overnight. Syriac texts suggest that the church leadership in the region was already facing internal challenges around this time, and the bishops of Beth Qatraye ceased attending synods in 674. While the practice of Christianity likely persisted in some pockets for a couple of centuries, the momentum had shifted decisively. The region's identity began to transform from a Syriac-speaking Christian outpost of the Sasanian world to an Arabic-speaking domain of the Islamic caliphate.

Following the death of the Prophet Muhammad in 632 CE, the new Islamic state faced a severe test in the form of the Ridda Wars, or Wars of Apostasy, as some tribes sought to break away from Medina's authority. The new Caliph, Abu Bakr, once again dispatched Al-Ala Al-Hadrami to the region to ensure its loyalty and suppress any rebellion. With the help of local tribes who remained true to their new faith, Al-Ala solidified Muslim control over the peninsula and the surrounding coast.

It was during this formative period of the Rashidun Caliphate (632-661) that the people of Qatar began to contribute directly to the expansion of the Islamic world. The inhabitants of the peninsula were renowned for their maritime skills, a legacy of centuries of fishing, pearling, and trade. This expertise was now put to new use. Historical records credit the seafaring Qataris with playing a valuable role in the formation and provision of the first Islamic naval fleet. This fleet was instrumental in transporting Muslim armies under the command of Al-Ala Al-Hadrami across the Gulf for the conquest of Persia, turning Qatar's coastline into a crucial launching point for the campaigns that would lead to the downfall of the Sasanian Empire.

When the center of Islamic power shifted to Damascus with the rise of the Umayyad Caliphate in 661, Qatar's role evolved. No longer a frontier zone in a war of conquest, it became an integrated, if remote, province of a vast and stable empire. The Umayyad era (661-750) was a time of commercial prosperity for the peninsula. Its strategic position in the Gulf made it a key stop on the maritime trade routes that now flourished under a unified political authority. The pearl banks, which had been harvested for millennia, grew in economic importance, with Qatari pearls becoming a prized commodity across the Caliphate.

Beyond the sea, the land itself offered another valuable resource. During the Umayyad period, Qatar became known as a center for breeding fine horses and camels, animals essential for trade, transport, and warfare across the expansive empire. This suggests a thriving pastoral economy in the interior, complementing the maritime activities of the coast. The combination of pearling, trade, and animal husbandry brought a new level of economic stability and connection to the wider world.

This era of integration was not without its turmoil. The Umayyad Caliphate faced numerous internal revolts, and the region of Qatar and Bahrain became a hotbed of activity for the Kharijites, an early Islamic sect known for its opposition to the ruling establishment. One of the most famous and formidable Khariji leaders was a man named Qatari ibn al-Fuja'a, whose very name indicates his origins in the peninsula. For more than a decade, he led a major revolt against the Umayyads, even holding the title of *Amir al-Mu'minin* (Commander of the Faithful) among his followers and minting his own coins. His rebellion, though ultimately unsuccessful, highlights that the people of the peninsula were not merely passive subjects but active, and at times defiant, participants in the major political and religious dramas of the day.

Archaeology provides tangible evidence of life in Umayyad Qatar. While many early Islamic sites have been identified, most are yet to be fully excavated. However, recent discoveries have begun to shed new light on this period. In the northwest of the country, a site known as Yoghbi has been identified as the earliest Islamic period settlement yet found in Qatar, with architectural features and ceramics dating back to the Umayyad period in the 7th and 8th centuries. The finds at Yoghbi and other nearby sites are significant because they suggest that settlement and economic activity in the Gulf during the early Islamic period were not solely dependent on the rise of major trade centers like Baghdad, but had their own local and regional dynamics.

Life in these early Islamic settlements was a blend of tradition and new influences. Excavations reveal simple stone-built houses, often arranged in small villages or clusters. The inhabitants continued to rely on the sea, as evidenced by the discovery of fishing tools, but their trade connections were now oriented towards the heartlands of the Caliphate. The discovery of ceramics from Iraq, alongside glass and metal fragments, points to a society that was part of the wider Umayyad economy, trading its local products for goods manufactured elsewhere in the empire. These scattered settlements represent a new chapter in Qatar's history: a settled, Arabic-speaking, and Muslim society, fully integrated into the political and economic life of one of the great empires of the age.

CHAPTER FOUR: The Abbasid Caliphate and the Rise of Local Powers

The year 750 CE marked a seismic shift in the Islamic world. In a bloody and decisive revolution, the Abbasid family, descendants of the Prophet Muhammad's uncle Abbas, overthrew the Damascus-based Umayyad Caliphate. The center of gravity of the empire swung eastward. The new caliphs established their capital first in Kufa, and then, in 762, founded a magnificent new circular city on the banks of the Tigris: Baghdad. This move was more than just a change of address; it was a reorientation of the empire. The focus shifted from the Mediterranean-facing provinces of Syria to the old Mesopotamian heartland, closer to the Abbasids' Persian power base. For the Qatar Peninsula and the wider Persian Gulf, this was a development of profound significance. Suddenly, they were no longer a remote eastern frontier but the maritime backyard of the world's new metropolis.

The founding of Baghdad unleashed an era of unprecedented prosperity and intellectual ferment known as the Islamic Golden Age. The city became a colossal consumer, a magnet for luxury goods, raw materials, and exotic commodities from across the known world. The Persian Gulf, which the Abbasids now firmly controlled, was its primary artery to the east. Ships sailing from Basra, the empire's main port, would stop at ports along the Gulf coast, including those in Qatar, before venturing on to India, Southeast Asia, and China. This integration into the Abbasid commercial network brought a new level of wealth and development to the peninsula. The most lucrative commodity Qatar had to offer was its pearls, whose luster was coveted in the opulent courts and bustling markets of Baghdad. While pearling was an ancient practice, the Abbasid era saw a substantial development in the industry, transforming it into a cornerstone of the local economy.

Archaeological evidence provides a vivid picture of this Abbasid-era boom. The most remarkable site is Murwab, located in the northwest of the peninsula, about 15 kilometers from the coast. Far from being a simple collection of huts, Murwab was the largest known early Islamic settlement in Qatar, a planned community that flourished in the 9th century. Excavations have revealed a sprawling site with the remains of over 250 stone-built houses, two mosques, and a substantial fort. This was not a temporary encampment but a permanent, sizable town, a rare window into life away from the coast during this period. The very existence of such a large inland settlement speaks to a degree of security and organization previously unseen.

At the heart of the settlement stood a rectangular fort, the oldest of its kind yet discovered in Qatar. It appears to have been a residence of some importance, perhaps for a local chieftain or an official representing the Caliphate's authority. The architecture of the fort and the layout of the settlement show clear Abbasid influences, linking the remote peninsula stylistically to the imperial center. The houses at Murwab, clustered together in groups, and the presence of two separate mosques suggest a well-ordered community. Life here was connected to a globalized economy. Shards of high-quality ceramics, including distinctive polychrome-glazed ware from Samarra—the temporary Abbasid capital in the 9th century—have been found in abundance. The discovery of Chinese porcelain and even West African coins demonstrates that goods from the farthest reaches of the Abbasid trade network were making their way to this corner of Qatar.

Murwab was clearly a center of some significance, but its prosperity, like that of the wider region, was intrinsically tied to the fortunes of the caliphs in Baghdad. By the late 9th century, the immense Abbasid Caliphate was beginning to show signs of stress. Political intrigue at court, the rising power of Turkic military commanders, and the vast expense of maintaining a sprawling empire began to erode the central government's authority. Revolts started to flare up in the provinces, and local dynasties began to assert their independence, withholding tax revenues from Baghdad. Eastern Arabia, including Qatar, was not immune to this turmoil. As early as 868, the region was a site of revolt against Abbasid rule. This weakening of central control created a power vacuum, and into that vacuum stepped one of the most radical and disruptive forces in Islamic history: the Qarmatians.

The Qarmatians were an extremist Isma'ili Shi'a sect that established a powerful, independent state centered in Al-Ahsa, in modern-day eastern Saudi Arabia, around 899 CE. They were more than just a breakaway dynasty; they were revolutionaries with a radical social and political agenda, sometimes described as a form of utopian socialism. They rejected the authority of both the Abbasid caliph in Baghdad and their Isma'ili rivals, the Fatimids in North Africa. For much of the 10th century, the Qarmatians were the dominant military power in the Persian Gulf and the Arabian Peninsula. Their influence was felt directly in Qatar, which fell under their sway.

Life under the Qarmatians was a stark departure from the stability of the early Abbasid era. They were fiercely militant, and their belief that the pilgrimage to Mecca was a superstition led them to launch devastating raids on pilgrim caravans. In 906, they ambushed a returning caravan and massacred 20,000 pilgrims. Their power reached its zenith in 930 when, under their charismatic leader Abu Tahir al-Jannabi, they committed an act that shocked the entire Muslim world: they sacked the holy city of Mecca. They slaughtered pilgrims in the sacred precincts, desecrated the holy well of Zamzam by filling it with corpses, and carried off the sacred Black Stone from the Kaaba to their capital.

This act of supreme sacrilege cemented their reputation as heretics and outcasts, but it also demonstrated their immense power. For years, they collected tribute from the Abbasid caliph himself. For the people of Qatar, the rise of the Qarmatians likely brought profound disruption. The lucrative pearl trade, dependent on stable maritime routes, would have been severely affected by the political instability and conflict. It is perhaps no coincidence that the abandonment of the prosperous settlement at Murwab seems to coincide with the beginning of the Qarmatian period in the late 9th century. The security and economic integration provided by the Abbasid empire had dissolved, replaced by the rule of a radical and unpredictable regional power.

The Qarmatian state, for all its military might, was not destined to last. A combination of internal divisions and external pressures gradually wore them down. By the latter half of the 11th century, their power was a shadow of its former self. A revolt on the island of Bahrain around 1058 heralded the final collapse of their authority. The final blow came from a local Arab dynasty, the Uyunids, who originated from the Banu Abdul Qays tribe of the Al-Ahsa region.

In 1077-1078, the Uyunid sheikh, Abdullah bin Ali Al Uyuni, secured military assistance from the powerful Seljuk Turks, who had by then taken over control of Baghdad from the Abbasids, and launched an uprising against the Qarmatians. He besieged the Qarmatian stronghold of Hofuf and, after a long struggle, defeated them, bringing their revolutionary state to an end. In its place, Abdullah bin Ali established the Uyunid Emirate, a new local power that would rule over eastern Arabia, including Qatar, for the next two centuries. The Uyunids restored a more conventional form of rule to the region, pledging allegiance to the Abbasid Caliphate in Baghdad and bringing an end to the long period of Qarmatian dominance. Their rise marked a new phase in the peninsula's history, where its fate would be determined not by distant imperial caliphs, but by the ambitions and rivalries of local Arab powers.

CHAPTER FIVE: The Age of Pearling and Trade: Qatar in the Medieval World

The end of the Qarmatian era in the late 11th century did not bring lasting stability to eastern Arabia, but rather a dizzying succession of local and regional dynasties, each vying for control of the lucrative trade routes and pearl banks of the Persian Gulf. For the inhabitants of the Qatar Peninsula, this was a period defined by shifting allegiances and the rise of distant powers whose ambitions dictated the rhythms of the local economy. Imperial Baghdad was a fading memory; the new centers of influence were Al-Ahsa, the island of Bahrain, and, above all, the fabulously wealthy port kingdom of Hormuz. Through it all, life on the peninsula revolved around one timeless, grueling, and all-consuming activity: the pearl harvest.

Following their victory over the Qarmatians in 1077, the Uyunids, an Arab dynasty from the Banu Abdul Qays tribe, established an emirate centered in Al-Ahsa that encompassed the Qatar Peninsula. For over a century and a half, they restored a semblance of conventional order to the region, nominally acknowledging the authority of the Abbasid caliphs. Under their rule, commerce revived and the Gulf's trade networks began to flourish once more. Their authority, however, was often contested, and by the mid-13th century, their power had crumbled. In 1253, they were overthrown by the Usfurids, another Arab dynasty from the Banu Uqayl, who in turn established their own regional emirate.

This period of flux saw the emergence of a new dominant force in the Gulf's maritime affairs: the Kingdom of Hormuz. Originally based on the Persian mainland, the rulers of Hormuz relocated their capital around 1301 to the barren island of Jarun, at the strategic mouth of the Gulf. This new island-fortress, which became known as Hormuz, was a masterstroke of geopolitical positioning. Though it had to import nearly all its food and even its fresh water, its location allowed it to become the indispensable tollgate for all maritime trade passing between the Indian Ocean and the ports of the Gulf. As one traveler famously noted, "the world is a ring, and Hormuz is the jewel in it."

The influence of Hormuz soon extended over the entire lower Gulf. Its rulers, through a combination of naval power and commercial acumen, established a network of vassal states that included ports in Oman, the islands of the Gulf, and the Arabian coastline. Qatar, with its valuable pearl banks, inevitably fell into this orbit. Local chieftains on the peninsula were obliged to pay tribute to the kings of Hormuz in exchange for protection and access to its vast trading network. This relationship transformed Qatari towns into vital cogs in a Hormuzi-dominated commercial machine, their pearls flowing into the markets of the island kingdom before being re-exported to destinations as far-flung as India, China, and eventually Europe. The great Moroccan traveler Ibn Battuta, who passed through the Gulf in the 1330s, described Hormuz as a bustling entrepôt, a meeting place for merchants from across the known world, painting a picture of the vibrant commercial environment into which Qatar was now integrated.

While dynasties rose and fell, the true ruler of life in Qatar was the annual pearling season, known as the *ghaus al-kabir*, or the "Great Dive." For four months every summer, from roughly June to September, the peninsula's society was fundamentally reordered. The majority of the able-bodied male population abandoned their coastal villages and took to the sea, leaving the towns in the care of women, children, and the elderly. This annual exodus was not merely an economic activity; it was the central organizing principle of the community, a shared experience of hardship, danger, and hope that shaped the culture for centuries.

The industry was built upon the dhow, the iconic wooden sailing vessel of the Arabian seas. These ships, with their distinctive lateen sails, were the workhorses of the Gulf, used for everything from fishing and trading to piracy. During the pearling season, hundreds of them would set out from ports like Al Huwailah, Fuwayrit, and the early settlements at Al Zubarah. Each boat was a microcosm of society, with a rigid hierarchy. At the top was the *nakhuda*, the captain, who was often the owner of the vessel and the financier of the expedition. Beneath him was a crew that could number from a dozen to over eighty men, each with a specific role.

The most vital and perilous job belonged to the *ghais*, the diver. The divers were the engine of the entire enterprise, their physical endurance the ultimate source of wealth. The work was brutally demanding. A typical day began shortly after sunrise and continued until sunset, with divers undertaking dozens of descents. Their equipment was starkly simple: a rope tied to a stone weighing several kilograms to speed their descent, a leather sheath to protect their fingers and toes from sharp coral, a woven basket to hold the oysters, and a bone or tortoiseshell clip called the *futtaim* to pinch their nostrils shut. Holding their breath for up to two minutes, they would descend to depths of over 18 meters, scraping as many oysters as they could from the seabed before being hauled back to the surface by their designated puller, the *saib*.

Life on the pearling dhows was one of extreme hardship. The men were crammed together on the deck for months, exposed to the searing summer sun. Fresh water was strictly rationed, and the diet consisted mainly of dates, rice, and fish. The work itself was fraught with danger. Divers faced the constant threat of sharks, barracudas, and venomous sea snakes. The repeated pressure changes took a toll on their bodies, often leading to hearing loss, respiratory problems, and other chronic ailments. Drowning was an ever-present risk. To endure the ordeal, the crews developed a rich oral culture of sea shanties and folk songs, their rhythmic chants providing a cadence for the grueling work and a sense of solidarity against the unforgiving sea.

The economic structure of the pearling industry was often exploitative. Most divers and pullers were bound by a system of debt peonage. Before the season began, the *nakhuda* would provide each crew member with an advance to support their families while they were away. This loan, along with the cost of their food and supplies for the journey, was recorded against their name. At the end of the season, the value of each man's share of the pearl catch was calculated and set against his debt. More often than not, the share was insufficient to clear the loan, trapping the diver in a cycle of debt that bound him to the same captain year after year, a system that would persist for generations.

Once the dhows returned to port, the next phase of the industry began. The thousands of collected oysters were opened on shore, a moment of great anticipation as the crew searched for the treasures within. The pearls were then sorted by size, color, shape, and luster. The most prized were the perfectly spherical, silvery-white pearls known as *jiwan*. These treasures were sold to the *tawawish*, the traveling pearl merchants, who would then take them to the major markets. Many of these merchants were agents for wealthy financiers in Bahrain, Basra, or increasingly, India. From the Gulf, Qatari pearls entered a global trade network, adorning the jewelry of royalty and nobility in Persia, the Ottoman Empire, and the princely courts of India.

Life on land in medieval Qatar was concentrated in a series of coastal villages and towns. Archaeological work has been limited for this specific period, but sites like Ruwayda have revealed fortifications and settlements that were active during this era. Life in these towns was modest. Dwellings were typically constructed from local materials—rough-hewn stone and gypsum mortar, with roofs made from mangrove poles and palm fronds. The layout of these towns was often organic, a cluster of houses and courtyards huddled around a central mosque and a well, with a defensive wall or fort providing protection from raids. While the men were at sea, women managed the households, raised the children, and often engaged in small-scale craft production, such as weaving.

For the people of the Qatar Peninsula, the medieval world was a place of both opportunity and constraint. Their lives were subject to the political machinations of regional powers and the economic dominance of powerful merchant cities like Hormuz. Yet, their unique skills as seafarers and their access to the rich pearl banks of the Gulf gave them an enduring and valuable role in the wider economy. It was an age defined by the iridescent shimmer of the pearl, a tiny object of beauty and desire that bound the small coastal communities of Qatar to the great currents of medieval world trade. This reliance on a single, precarious commodity would define the peninsula's destiny for the next four hundred years, a period that would begin with the jarring arrival of strange new ships on the horizon, bearing the flags of a distant European power.

CHAPTER SIX: The Portuguese and Ottoman Sway: A Contest for the Gulf

For the dhow captains and pearl merchants of the Qatar Peninsula, the dawn of the 16th century looked much like the centuries that had preceded it. Their world was framed by the rhythms of the monsoon winds and the pearling season, their fortunes tied to the great mercantile kingdom of Hormuz, the jewel of the Gulf. Local chieftains paid tribute to the Hormuzi kings, and in return, their pearls, dried fish, and Arabian horses entered a vibrant trade network that stretched from Basra to India. This familiar world, governed by local alliances and ancient commercial ties, was about to be shattered by the arrival of outsiders whose ships, cannons, and ambitions were unlike anything the Gulf had ever seen.

In 1507, a Portuguese squadron of seven ships and about 500 men, commanded by the formidable Afonso de Albuquerque, sliced through the waters of the Gulf of Oman. Their mission, part of a grand strategy devised by King Manuel I of Portugal, was ruthlessly simple: to seize control of the key arteries of the Indian Ocean trade. By capturing strategic choke points like Aden at the mouth of the Red Sea, Malacca in Southeast Asia, and Hormuz at the entrance to the Persian Gulf, Portugal intended to break the centuries-old monopoly held by Muslim merchants and redirect the fabulous wealth of the spice trade directly to Lisbon. Albuquerque's methods were brutal and efficient. Sweeping up the Omani coast, he stormed and sacked the towns of Qalhat, Qurayyat, and Muscat before setting his sights on the ultimate prize: Hormuz itself.

The attack on Hormuz was a shocking display of European naval firepower. The Portuguese warships, armed with rows of cannons, easily outmatched the vast but technologically inferior fleet defending the island kingdom. Hormuz was compelled to submit, its ruler becoming a vassal of the Portuguese crown and agreeing to pay a hefty annual tribute. A mutiny among his captains forced Albuquerque to temporarily abandon the prize, but he returned in force in 1515, crushing all resistance and cementing Portuguese control. He immediately began construction of a massive fortress, the Fort of Our Lady of the Conception, its stone walls rising as an unambiguous statement of a new order. Hormuz, once the independent jewel of the Gulf, was now the lynchpin of Portugal's *Estado da Índia*, its eastern empire.

For Qatar and the other Arabian coastal settlements, the fall of Hormuz was a cataclysm. Their political and economic overlord was now a European Christian power. The Portuguese system was extractive. They were not interested in colonization in the traditional sense, but in control. All local ships were required to purchase a Portuguese license, or *cartaz*, to engage in trade. Refusal meant the confiscation of cargo or the sinking of the vessel. The lucrative pearl trade, the lifeblood of Qatar's coastal communities, was now subject to Portuguese taxation and control, channeled through their new customs houses at Hormuz and, after its conquest by a Portuguese-Hormuzi force in 1521, Bahrain.

The Portuguese presence in Qatar itself was indirect. There is no definitive evidence that they ever built forts on the peninsula or maintained a permanent garrison there. Their strategy was to control the major hubs of Bahrain and Hormuz, from which they could dominate the entire southern Gulf. The name "Qatar" appears on 16th-century Portuguese maps, and their chroniclers mention the peninsula, but it remained a periphery to their main interests. The local sheikhs were likely compelled to deal with the new reality, paying tribute to the Portuguese governor in Bahrain or Hormuz rather than to an independent Hormuzi king, their pearling fleets operating under the watchful eye of Portuguese patrols.

Just as the Portuguese were consolidating their maritime empire, a new superpower was rising to their north. The Ottoman Empire, having conquered Constantinople in 1453, was in a period of dramatic expansion. Under Sultan Selim I, the Ottomans defeated the Mamluks of Egypt in 1517, bringing the holy cities of Mecca and Medina and the vital Red Sea trade routes under their control. His successor, Suleiman the Magnificent, continued the push eastward, capturing Baghdad from the Persian Safavids in 1534. By 1538, the Ottomans had reached Basra at the head of the Persian Gulf. The stage was now set for a direct confrontation between the two empires. The Persian Gulf had become a frontier in a global contest for supremacy.

The Ottoman-Portuguese rivalry was a clash of titans. The Ottomans, the preeminent land power, saw the Portuguese as infidel intruders disrupting the traditional pilgrimage and trade routes. The Portuguese, masters of the sea, viewed the Ottomans as their primary strategic and commercial rivals in the Indian Ocean. The conflict played out in a series of naval campaigns, raids, and sieges across the region. In 1538, a large Ottoman fleet sailed from Suez to besiege the Portuguese fortress at Diu in India, but the attempt failed.

The most notable Ottoman commander in the region was the celebrated admiral and cartographer Piri Reis. In 1552, Piri Reis led a fleet from Suez with the objective of capturing Hormuz. He successfully sacked the Portuguese-held port of Muscat but failed to take the main fortress at Hormuz. After a brief occupation of the town, he withdrew his fleet to Basra upon hearing of an approaching Portuguese relief force. This indecisive outcome led to his tragic downfall; he was executed in Egypt on the orders of the Sultan, accused of failing in his mission. Subsequent Ottoman naval actions in the Gulf, including a disastrous defeat in the Strait of Hormuz in 1553 and a failed attempt to take Bahrain in 1559, confirmed Portuguese naval superiority in the open sea.

Unable to dislodge the Portuguese from their key island fortresses, the Ottomans shifted their strategy to consolidating control over the Arabian mainland. In the mid-16th century, they formally established the Eyalet of Lahsa (Al-Ahsa), a new province administered from the oasis city of Hofuf. This move was primarily intended to protect Basra's trade and to serve as a bulwark against Portuguese raids. The new province officially encompassed the lands of the Qatar Peninsula. For the first time, Qatar was formally incorporated, at least on paper, into the administrative structure of the Ottoman Empire.

In reality, Ottoman sway over the peninsula was likely light. Istanbul's primary concern was securing the major towns of Al-Ahsa and Qatif and collecting taxes. Direct administration of the remote and sparsely populated Qatari coast would have been impractical and of little strategic value. The local tribal leaders probably acknowledged Ottoman suzerainty, perhaps paying nominal tribute to the Pasha in Al-Ahsa, but largely continued to govern their own affairs. Life remained centered on the sea, though now the pearling and fishing boats operated in waters contested by the navies of two distant empires. One source suggests that the Ottoman admiral Piri Reis occupied the Qatar peninsula for a time to deny the Portuguese a potential base, but this control was likely fleeting.

By the turn of the 17th century, the foundations of Portuguese power in the Gulf were beginning to crack. A century of over-extension, corruption, and the constant need to defend a vast network of far-flung fortresses had taken its toll. New and formidable European rivals had arrived in the Indian Ocean: the English and Dutch East India Companies. These new arrivals were better capitalized and more ruthlessly focused on commerce. Simultaneously, a resurgent Safavid Persia under the powerful Shah Abbas I was determined to reclaim its territory.

The decisive blow came in 1622. Shah Abbas, who lacked a navy, forged an alliance with the English East India Company. English ships bombarded the fort at Hormuz and transported Persian troops to the island. After a ten-week siege, the Portuguese garrison surrendered. The fall of Hormuz after more than a century of Portuguese rule was a landmark event that completely changed the balance of power in the Gulf. The Portuguese were forced to retreat to Muscat and other Omani ports, their era of dominance shattered.

The expulsion of the Portuguese did not, however, lead to a reassertion of direct Ottoman control over the entire Arabian coast. The Ottomans themselves were facing internal challenges and costly wars in Europe. Their grip on the Lahsa province had always been tenuous, challenged by the powerful Bedouin tribes of the interior. The primary beneficiaries of the power vacuum left by the Portuguese were not the Ottomans or the Persians, but local Arab powers.

In the 1660s, the powerful Bani Khalid tribal confederation, based in Al-Ahsa, rose in revolt. Under their leader, Barrak ibn Ghurayr, they defeated the Ottoman garrisons and, by 1670, had expelled them from Hofuf, establishing their own independent emirate. The Bani Khalid Emirate would dominate eastern Arabia, including Qatar, for more than a century. For the people of the Qatar Peninsula, the distant authority of the Ottoman Pasha in Al-Ahsa was replaced by the more immediate and culturally familiar authority of the Bani Khalid sheikhs. The great imperial contest between Lisbon and Istanbul had faded, replaced by a new era in which the peninsula's destiny would be shaped by the rising tribal confederations of Arabia. It was from within this new political landscape that the families who would found the modern Gulf states, including the Al Thani, would begin their ascent.

CHAPTER SEVEN: The Rise of the Al Thani: The Foundation of Modern Qatar

The 18th century dawned on a Persian Gulf transformed. The grand imperial contest between the Ottomans and the Portuguese had receded, leaving a mosaic of local powers to fill the void. In eastern Arabia, the dominant force was the Bani Khalid tribal confederation, which held sway over a vast territory stretching from Kuwait to the borders of Qatar. Inland, a formidable new power was stirring in the heart of the Nejd: the Emirate of Diriyah, a potent alliance between the political ambition of Muhammad ibn Saud and the puritanical Islamic revivalism of Muhammad ibn Abd al-Wahhab. This volatile landscape, a patchwork of tribal loyalties and nascent states, set the stage for a period of migration and realignment that would reshape the Qatar Peninsula and witness the quiet arrival of a family destined to forge a nation.

The peninsula, with its long coastline and rich pearl banks, acted as a magnet for tribes seeking opportunity or refuge from the conflicts of the interior. Among the most significant arrivals was a section of the Utub tribal confederation, a powerful alliance of clans from the Nejd. By the 1760s, a branch of the Utub, the Al Khalifa, had migrated from Kuwait and settled on the northwest coast of Qatar, founding a new town that would quickly become the peninsula's commercial heart: Al Zubarah.

Al Zubarah's growth was nothing short of meteoric. Built around a deep natural harbour and protected by formidable defensive walls, its rise was fueled by a deliberate policy of free trade and security that attracted merchants from as far away as Basra, Persia, and India. After the Persian occupation of Basra in 1777, a flood of merchants and their families relocated to the booming town. Al Zubarah became one of the Gulf's premier centers for the pearl trade, its markets bustling with activity and its wealth attracting both admiration and envy. It was a testament to the commercial energy of the Gulf Arabs, a thriving city-state built on pearling and global trade, whose remains are now a UNESCO World Heritage site.

It was into this dynamic environment that the ancestors of the Al Thani family arrived. A branch of the Ma'adhid tribe, who in turn trace their lineage to the great Banu Tamim tribe of central Arabia, they had migrated from the Jabrin oasis. Historical sources trace their movements from the south of the peninsula to the north, stopping at Ruwais and eventually settling in the coastal town of Fuwayrit. Here, under the leadership of their patriarch, Thani bin Mohammed, the family established itself within the pearling and fishing economy of the town. Life was dictated by the seasons of the sea, and a family's standing was built on reputation, piety, and the ability to navigate the complex web of tribal relationships.

In Fuwayrit, Thani's son, Mohammed, was born around the year 1776. Mohammed bin Thani would grow to become a man known for his wisdom, patience, and diplomatic skill, qualities that would serve him well in the turbulent decades to come. He rose to become the chief of his tribe in Fuwayrit, a local leader of growing stature in a land that still had no central authority. Each town and tribe had its own sheikh, and while they shared a common culture, they were often rivals, their loyalties shifting with the political tides. The notion of a unified Qatar did not yet exist.

A pivotal event in 1783 sent shockwaves across the region and directly impacted the peninsula. The Al Khalifa, leading a coalition of Utub tribes from their base in Al Zubarah, launched a successful invasion of the nearby island of Bahrain, driving out the Persian garrison. This conquest was a major turning point. The Al Khalifa soon moved their primary seat of power from Al Zubarah to Bahrain, establishing a new dynastic sheikhdom. From their new capital in Manama, they now claimed authority not only over Bahrain but also over the Qatar Peninsula, viewing Al Zubarah and its hinterland as a dependency.

This claim was a source of constant friction for the next eight decades. The Al Khalifa sought to extract taxes from the wealthy pearling towns of Qatar and treated the peninsula's inhabitants as subjects. The proudly independent tribes of Qatar, however, bridled under this external rule. This simmering resentment was exacerbated by the presence of a Bahraini political representative in Qatar, whose often harsh rule generated widespread animosity. The situation was further complicated by the waxing and waning power of the Saudis, who periodically exerted their own influence over the peninsula, collecting religious tithes and challenging Al Khalifa authority. The political landscape was a treacherous triangle of competing interests: the Al Khalifa in Bahrain, the Wahhabi emirs in the Nejd, and the fiercely independent tribes on the peninsula itself.

Amidst this instability, the tribes of Qatar looked for leaders who could represent their interests and provide a focus for their shared identity. By the 1840s, Mohammed bin Thani had emerged as just such a figure. In 1848, he took a decisive step, relocating his family and followers from the northern town of Fuwayrit to Al Bida, the settlement that would later grow into the city of Doha. In Doha, his influence grew, and by 1851 he was recognized as the ruler of the town. He was not yet the ruler of all Qatar, but he was a respected elder and a skillful negotiator, adept at playing his powerful neighbors off against one another. He forged a tactical alliance with the Saudi emir, Faisal bin Turki, who visited him in Qatar in 1851, strengthening his position against the Al Khalifa.

Throughout the 1850s and 1860s, Mohammed bin Thani carefully consolidated his authority. While other formidable figures plied the waters of the Gulf, such as the famous pirate-turned-privateer Rahmah ibn Jabir al-Jalahimah, who for a time was the most powerful tribal leader on the peninsula, Mohammed bin Thani built his power base through diplomacy and consensus. He patiently worked to unify the often-warring Qatari tribes, reminding them of their common interests in the face of external threats.

The long-simmering tensions with Bahrain finally boiled over into open war in 1867. The ruler of Bahrain, Sheikh Mohammed bin Khalifa Al Khalifa, allied himself with Sheikh Zayed bin Khalifa of Abu Dhabi. In October of that year, they launched a massive joint naval expedition against Qatar. The combined Bahraini and Abu Dhabi forces sacked the towns of Doha and Al Wakrah with devastating effect. Contemporary accounts describe wide-scale destruction, with houses dismantled, inhabitants deported, and significant loss of life.

The tribes of Qatar, led by Mohammed bin Thani's energetic son, Jassim, rallied for a counterattack. Though they suffered a defeat at sea, they managed to defend their positions on land, even capturing two of the Bahraini commanders before a prisoner exchange was negotiated. The war had reached a bloody stalemate, but the sheer violence of the assault had crossed a critical line. The attack was a flagrant violation of the 1835 General Maritime Treaty, an agreement policed by Great Britain to ensure the security of its trade routes to India. The British, who had until this point largely considered Qatar a dependency of Bahrain, were now forced to intervene directly.

The man tasked with resolving the crisis was the British Political Resident in the Persian Gulf, Colonel Lewis Pelly. A firm and decisive agent of the British Raj, Pelly sailed to the region in 1868 with a clear mission: to punish the violators of the maritime truce and restore stability. He held the ruler of Bahrain directly responsible for the aggression, deposed him, and installed his brother Ali in his place. Pelly then made a decision that would change the course of Qatari history. Instead of dealing with Qatar through the new ruler of Bahrain, he sailed directly to the coast of Qatar to negotiate with its leaders.

This act was, in itself, a revolution. For the first time, a major external power was treating the sheikhs of Qatar as a separate and distinct political entity. Pelly summoned the peninsula's leading men, who chose the elderly and widely respected Mohammed bin Thani to be their representative. On September 12, 1868, Mohammed bin Thani and Colonel Lewis Pelly signed a historic agreement. In the treaty, Mohammed bin Thani agreed that the people of Qatar would not disturb the peace of the sea and would refer all future disputes to the British Resident. In return, the

British implicitly recognized Qatar's distinctness from Bahrain and explicitly acknowledged Mohammed bin Thani as its leader.

The Anglo-Qatari Agreement of 1868 was the birth certificate of the modern Qatari state. It did not grant full independence, but it severed the long-contested legal and political link to Bahrain. It formally acknowledged a single leader for the people of the peninsula, providing a focal point for the development of a unified political identity. Mohammed bin Thani, the patient sheikh from Fuwayrit, had successfully navigated decades of regional conflict and tribal rivalries to lay the cornerstone of a new state. By securing this crucial international recognition, he had set the stage for his son, Jassim, to build upon this foundation and forge a truly independent and unified nation.

CHAPTER EIGHT: Sheikh Jassim bin Mohammed Al Thani: Unifier and Founder

The Anglo-Qatari Agreement of 1868 was a quiet revolution. With the stroke of a pen, a British colonel and an elderly tribal sheikh had redrawn the political map of the lower Gulf, acknowledging Qatar as a distinct entity and Mohammed bin Thani as its leader. But a treaty on paper is one thing; forging a nation from a disparate collection of fiercely independent towns and tribes is quite another. That monumental task would fall to Sheikh Mohammed's eldest son, Jassim, a man whose character seemed purpose-built for the turbulent era into which he was born. Where his father was a patient diplomat who navigated threats through careful negotiation, Jassim was a warrior, a poet, and a devoutly religious man whose instinct was to confront challenges head-on.

Born around 1825, Jassim bin Mohammed Al Thani was raised in the northern town of Fuwayrit, schooled in the Quran, Islamic jurisprudence, and the traditional Arab arts of horsemanship and falconry. He came of age in a world of constant conflict and shifting allegiances. By the time he moved with his father to Al Bida (Doha) as a young man of twenty-one, he had already proven himself a capable leader, commanding Qatari forces in the defense of the peninsula. He was the driving force behind the Qatari counter-attacks during the devastating 1867 war with Bahrain and Abu Dhabi, and his leadership on the battlefield had earned him the respect of the tribes. When his aging father formally passed the mantle of leadership to him on December 18, 1878—a date now celebrated as Qatar's National Day—Jassim inherited a land whose separate status was recognized, but whose security was far from guaranteed.

Jassim's primary challenge was strategic. The 1868 treaty with Great Britain secured Qatar from aggression by sea, effectively neutralizing the naval threat from Bahrain. Britain's imperial navy policed the Gulf, and no local power dared challenge it. The land, however, was another matter entirely. The treaty offered no protection from attack by land, leaving Qatar's long, porous border vulnerable to its powerful and often hostile neighbors in the Nejd and Abu Dhabi. Jassim, deeply pragmatic and wary of becoming wholly dependent on a Christian European power, concluded that he needed to balance one empire against another. He needed an ally on land, a fellow Islamic power that could deter his rivals. He turned his gaze north, to the resurgent Ottoman Empire.

In 1871, the energetic Ottoman governor of Baghdad, Midhat Pasha, was in the process of reasserting the Sultan's authority in eastern Arabia. Seeing an opportunity, Sheikh Jassim extended an invitation. An Ottoman envoy arrived from Kuwait bearing four flags, symbols of the Sultan's suzerainty. Jassim accepted one and hoisted it over his house in Doha. By December 1871, a detachment of 100 Ottoman troops and a field gun under the command of Major Ömer Bey had arrived and established a garrison in the fort at Al Bida. In January 1872, Qatar was formally incorporated into the Ottoman Empire as a *kaza*, or district, within the Sanjak of Nejd. Sheikh Jassim was appointed its *kaymakam*, or sub-governor.

On the surface, the arrangement seemed ideal for Jassim. He had secured a powerful Muslim ally to protect his landward flank, and in return, he received an official title and recognition from Istanbul that further legitimized his rule. The Ottomans, for their part, gained a strategic foothold on the Arabian coast, extending their influence and vexing their British rivals. For a time, the alliance worked. The presence of the Ottoman garrison brought a measure of stability, and under the new arrangement, the pearl trade boomed, enhancing Doha's status as a commercial hub.

However, the political honeymoon was short-lived. The alliance, which Jassim viewed as a partnership of convenience, was seen very differently in Istanbul. The Ottomans, in the midst of their Tanzimat reform era, were attempting to centralize their sprawling empire and began to treat Qatar less like an autonomous sheikhdom and more like a regular province. Friction was inevitable. The first major source of conflict arose when the Ottomans, accustomed to direct taxation, attempted to establish a customs house in Doha. This was a direct threat to Sheikh Jassim's authority and his primary source of revenue. He and the other Qatari sheikhs had always controlled the pearling taxes, and the Ottoman attempt to usurp this role was a challenge to their economic and political power.

Relations deteriorated further over the next decade. The Ottomans offered no help when Jassim was embroiled in a long-running conflict with Abu Dhabi over the territory of Khor Al Adaid. By the mid-1880s, Ottoman officials were receiving complaints from some Qataris about Sheikh Jassim's allegedly oppressive rule and even supported a rival, an Ottoman subject named Mohammed bin Abdul Wahab, who tried to supplant Jassim as *kaymakam* in 1888. The Sheikh repeatedly tried to resign his post in protest, at one point retiring to the coastal village of Al Daayen and declaring he was no longer responsible for the administration of the country. The Ottomans were no longer the helpful counterweight Jassim had sought; they were becoming a burden, a rival authority within his own land. By August 1892, he had stopped paying taxes to the empire altogether.

The final rupture came with the arrival of a new, hardline governor of Basra, Mehmed Hafiz Pasha. Determined to bring the defiant sheikh to heel, the governor sailed to Qatar in February 1893 with a force of around 200 soldiers and additional reinforcements on the way. Jassim, now an old man in his late sixties and fearing imprisonment or death, refused to meet the governor, citing ill health. He withdrew from Doha, gathering his supporters—a formidable force of Bedouin and townsmen numbering between 3,000 and 4,000—and took up a defensive position at the Al Wajbah fort, about 15 kilometers west of the city.

Frustrated by Jassim's defiance, Mehmed Hafiz Pasha lost his patience. In March, he summoned Jassim's younger brother, Sheikh Ahmed bin Mohammed Al Thani, along with more than a dozen other prominent Qatari leaders, for negotiations. When they arrived, he had them arrested and imprisoned on his corvette, the *Merrikh*, anchored in the bay. This act of treachery was the spark that ignited the conflict. It was an intolerable insult to the honor of the Al Thani and the tribes of Qatar. When the governor rejected Jassim's offer of 10,000 liras for the release of the hostages, war became unavoidable.

Mehmed Hafiz Pasha dispatched a column of troops under the command of his general, Yusuf Effendi, with orders to march on Al Wajbah and crush Jassim's rebellion. The Ottomans, with their modern rifles and military discipline, likely expected an easy victory over what they perceived as a simple tribal rabble. They had catastrophically underestimated their opponent and his deep connection to the land.

As Yusuf Effendi's column advanced into the desert, they were lured into an ambush. Sheikh Jassim's forces, composed of cavalry and infantry, used their intimate knowledge of the terrain to devastating effect. Concealed in the depressions and behind the low hills surrounding Al Wajbah, they opened a withering fire on the exposed Ottoman soldiers. The battle raged for hours, but the outcome was never in doubt. The surprised and beleaguered Ottoman column broke and retreated first to the nearby Shebaka fort, and then all the way back to their main fort in Doha, sustaining heavy casualties along the way.

The victory was total and humiliating for the Ottomans. Jassim's forces advanced on Doha, laying siege to the fort and, crucially, cutting off its water supply. Trapped, thirsty, and with no hope of relief, the Ottoman garrison conceded defeat. A deal was struck: the Qatari hostages, including Sheikh Ahmed, would be released in exchange for allowing the governor's cavalry safe passage back to the mainland.

The Battle of Al Wajbah, fought in March 1893, was the defining moment in the foundation of the modern Qatari state. It was a stunning military victory that demonstrated the unity of the Qatari tribes under Al Thani leadership and their determination to resist external domination. When news of the fiasco reached Istanbul, Sultan Abdul Hamid II acted swiftly. Mehmed Hafiz Pasha was dismissed as governor of Basra, and a full pardon was issued to Sheikh Jassim. The Ottomans had learned a costly lesson.

In the aftermath of the battle, a new, unwritten understanding emerged. The Ottoman garrison remained in Doha, and the Ottoman flag still flew over the fort, but their authority beyond its walls had evaporated. They were guests, not rulers. Sheikh Jassim was the undisputed master of the peninsula, his authority now cemented by a historic military victory. The British, who had watched the conflict with keen interest, also took note. They had tried to mediate, and Jassim had even offered to place Qatar under their protection, but they had been unable to intervene decisively. Now, it was clear to all that effective power in Qatar lay with one man.

Sheikh Jassim bin Mohammed Al Thani spent his final years living peacefully in Lusail, a village north of Doha, having delegated the day-to-day running of the country to his brother, Sheikh Ahmed. He had successfully navigated the treacherous currents of imperial rivalry, playing the British and Ottomans against each other to preserve his country's autonomy. More importantly, he had rallied the tribes of the peninsula, from the coastal towns to the desert interior, uniting them in a common struggle against an outside power and, in the process, forging a nascent national identity. He was a scholar, a warrior, a canny statesman, and a poet who chronicled the exploits of his people. When he died on July 17, 1913, he left behind a unified and coherent political entity, a proto-state that had successfully asserted its right to exist. He was, in every sense, the founder of Qatar.

CHAPTER NINE: The Anglo-Qatari Treaty of 1916: A New Era of Protection

The death of Sheikh Jassim bin Mohammed Al Thani on July 17, 1913, marked the end of an era. For four decades, his formidable personality had been the gravitational center of the peninsula, binding its fractious tribes into a coherent whole through force of will, shrewd diplomacy, and a landmark military victory. He had successfully balanced the competing ambitions of the British and Ottoman empires, preserving a hard-won autonomy. Now, the unifier was gone. The question of what would come next hung heavy in the humid air of Doha.

The mantle of leadership passed to Sheikh Jassim's fourth son, Abdullah bin Jassim Al Thani. Born in Doha around 1880, Abdullah was a different man from his warrior father. Where Jassim was impetuous and confrontational, Abdullah was known for his piety, patience, and preference for negotiation over conflict. His father had groomed him for this role, appointing him governor of Doha in 1906 and relying on him as a trusted deputy. The succession was peaceful, a testament to the respect Abdullah commanded, but the challenges he inherited were immense. He was now the leader of a land whose independence was de facto, but not de jure, and whose security rested on a delicate and rapidly changing geopolitical balance. The most visible symbol of this ambiguity was the continued presence of the Ottoman garrison in their fort at Al Bida, a remnant of an imperial authority that had long since faded in reality but still existed on paper.

Even as Sheikh Abdullah took power, the tectonic plates of global politics were shifting beneath his feet. Just twelve days after his accession, on July 29, 1913, diplomats from the British and Ottoman empires signed a document in London that directly concerned his future. The Anglo-Ottoman Convention of 1913 was a grand imperial bargain, an attempt by the two powers to neatly delineate their spheres of influence across the Persian Gulf and Arabia. Its articles dealt with the status of Kuwait, the borders of

Nejd, and the affairs of Bahrain. Crucially, one section addressed Qatar. The Ottomans, in exchange for British concessions elsewhere, formally renounced all their claims of sovereignty over the peninsula and agreed to withdraw their garrison from Doha. The British, in turn, promised not to annex Qatar and to uphold the autonomy of its ruler. The agreement, had it been ratified, would have been a peaceful and tidy resolution to the peninsula's ambiguous status.

History, however, is rarely tidy. The ink on the convention was barely dry when events in Europe rendered it obsolete. The assassination of an Austrian archduke in Sarajevo in June 1914 triggered a cascade of alliances and ultimatums that, by August, had plunged the continent into the Great War. In October, the Ottoman Empire, having cast its lot with Germany and the Central Powers, officially entered the conflict against Great Britain and its allies. The Ottoman garrison in Doha was no longer the token presence of a fading, sometimes-ally; it was now an enemy outpost on a coastline vital to the security of British India.

For Sheikh Abdullah, the outbreak of war presented both a crisis and an opportunity. His pro-British inclinations were well known, but the Ottomans were fellow Muslims, and the Sultan in Istanbul still held the title of Caliph, a potent symbol for many in the Islamic world. He had to tread carefully. The Ottoman garrison, though isolated and dwindling in number as men deserted, was still a physical presence in his capital. The British, meanwhile, were applying pressure. Their naval supremacy in the Gulf was absolute, and they now viewed the Ottoman fort with deep suspicion.

The situation came to a head in August 1915. Two British warships, HMS *Pyramus* and HMS *Dalhousie*, appeared off the coast of Doha. The British Political Agent from Bahrain, Major T.H. Keyes, came ashore to "fetch" Sheikh Abdullah for a meeting. The message, delivered under the guns of the Royal Navy, was unmistakable. Keyes's official mission was to search for dhows belonging to hostile tribesmen, but his real purpose, under instructions from the chief British political officer in the

Gulf, Sir Percy Cox, was to resolve the matter of the Ottoman garrison. Cox had authorized Keyes to offer Sheikh Abdullah a financial incentive for each artillery piece he could secure from the fort.

The endgame was swift. Faced with the reality of British naval power, cut off from any hope of reinforcement, and likely persuaded by Sheikh Abdullah, the last Ottoman troops recognized the futility of their position. On the night of August 19, 1915, they quietly abandoned the Al Bida fort and slipped away. The next morning, a British landing party found the fort deserted. They seized a small cache of weapons and ammunition, including one mountain gun and two field guns whose breechblocks had been removed. After 44 years, the last vestiges of Ottoman authority in Qatar were gone. Sheikh Abdullah, having assisted the British, was rewarded with the captured military stores and a payment in rupees.

The withdrawal of the Ottomans left a power vacuum. While Qatar was now free of any foreign troops for the first time in decades, it was also exposed. Sheikh Jassim had used the Ottoman presence as a strategic counterweight to British influence and a deterrent against land-based attacks from his Arabian rivals. Now, that deterrent was gone. To the west, the ambitious and formidable Abdulaziz Ibn Saud was rapidly consolidating his power in the Nejd, and his territorial aspirations were a source of constant concern for all the coastal rulers. Without a powerful protector, Qatar's hard-won autonomy felt fragile. Sheikh Abdullah, a pragmatist like his father, knew he had to make a choice. The only power capable of guaranteeing his sheikhdom's security was Great Britain.

The British, for their part, were eager to formalize the relationship. The war had underscored the strategic importance of the Gulf, and their policy was to bring all the coastal sheikhdoms into a unified system of treaties, ensuring no other European power could gain a foothold. With the Ottomans gone, the path was clear to bring Qatar, the last of the coastal states without such a treaty, into what was known as the Trucial System of Administration.

Negotiations began between Sheikh Abdullah and the architect of British policy in the region, Sir Percy Cox. A seasoned and imposing figure of British India's political service, Cox was known for his deep understanding of the region and his ability to forge relationships with its rulers. The negotiations were not entirely straightforward. Sheikh Abdullah was determined to secure the best possible terms for his country. He wanted a clear and unambiguous guarantee of protection, not just from attacks by sea—which the Royal Navy could easily provide—but also from the much more likely threat of attack by land.

This was a traditional sticking point for the British. Their imperial strategy was based on maritime power, and they were deeply reluctant to be drawn into complex and costly tribal disputes in the Arabian interior. Committing British troops to defend a desert frontier was a quagmire they had always sought to avoid. Sheikh Abdullah also had reservations about clauses that he felt encroached on Qatar's sovereignty, particularly those that would permit British nationals to compete in the pearl trade and allow for the establishment of a British political agent and post office in Doha.

Despite these points of contention, the overarching logic of the alliance was inescapable for both sides. After extensive discussions, a final agreement was reached. On November 3, 1916, aboard a British vessel off the coast, Sheikh Abdullah bin Jassim Al Thani and Sir Percy Cox signed the Anglo-Qatari Treaty.

The treaty, composed of eleven articles, fundamentally reshaped Qatar's place in the world. It followed the template of the other "exclusive agreements" Britain had with the Gulf sheikhdoms. Sheikh Abdullah pledged not to enter into any relationship with any other foreign power without British consent. He likewise agreed not to cede, sell, or mortgage any part of his territory to any other power and promised not to grant any economic concessions without British approval. The treaty also reaffirmed his commitment to suppressing the slave trade and piracy.

In return, Britain offered its protection. The key articles mirrored the delicate negotiations. The British government promised to protect Qatar from "all aggression by sea." On the crucial issue of a land attack, the language was more circumspect. Britain did not promise direct military intervention but pledged to provide its "good offices," a diplomatic term meaning it would use its influence and mediation to assist the ruler—a weaker guarantee than Abdullah had hoped for, but a significant commitment nonetheless. The treaty also formally recognized Abdullah as the legitimate ruler of Qatar and extended this recognition to his heirs and successors, thereby solidifying the Al Thani dynasty's position under the shield of the British Empire.

The Anglo-Qatari Treaty of 1916 was the third great pillar in the foundation of the modern state, following the 1868 agreement that established Qatar's distinctness from Bahrain and the 1893 Battle of Al Wajbah that confirmed its autonomy from the Ottomans. It ended the long era of strategic ambiguity and formally integrated Qatar into the British imperial sphere of influence, a relationship that would define its political existence for the next fifty-five years. Sheikh Abdullah, through quiet and patient diplomacy, had navigated the collapse of one empire and the ascendancy of another, securing for his vulnerable sheikhdom the protection of the world's greatest naval power. In the midst of a world war that was redrawing maps across the Middle East, he had ensured Qatar's survival and laid the political groundwork for its future.

CHAPTER TEN: The Great Depression and the Decline of the Pearl Industry

In the early 1920s, life in Qatar, now a British protectorate, followed a rhythm that would have been familiar to a Qatari grandfather or even a great-grandfather. The world outside had been convulsed by a Great War, empires had vanished, and new technologies were changing the face of modern life, but the peninsula's existence still revolved around the four-month agony and ecstasy of the pearling season. The *ghaus al-kabir* was more than an industry; it was the metronome of society. It dictated the calendar, governed the economy, and defined the social order. Nearly the entire male population was involved in some capacity. Wealth and status were measured in the luster and size of the pearls brought up from the depths. Sheikh Abdullah bin Jassim's government, like that of his forebears, derived its modest revenues from taxes on the pearling fleet. While the 1916 treaty with Britain provided external security, internal prosperity depended entirely on this single, iridescent commodity.

The industry had experienced booms and busts before, subject to the whims of weather, disease in the oyster beds, and fluctuations in faraway markets. A price spike during World War I, for instance, had brought a brief period of inflated prosperity. But no one in the bustling pearling towns of Doha, Al Wakrah, or Fuwayrit could have possibly imagined that this entire way of life, honed over centuries, was about to be rendered obsolete with breathtaking speed. The collapse, when it came, was not the result of a single cause but a perfect storm of technological innovation from halfway around the world and an economic cataclysm that began in the canyons of Wall Street.

The first, and most decisive, blow came not from a rival navy or a regional competitor, but from a laboratory in Japan. For decades, a Japanese entrepreneur named Mikimoto Kōkichi had been obsessed with replicating the natural process of pearl creation. After years of painstaking experimentation, he perfected a method of implanting a tiny bead of mother-of-pearl into a living oyster, tricking the mollusk into coating the irritant with layers of nacre. The result was a "cultured" pearl, physically and chemically almost identical to its natural counterpart. By the early 1920s, Mikimoto's process was becoming commercially viable, and by the middle of the decade, round, lustrous cultured pearls were beginning to appear on the world market.

The initial reaction in the Gulf was a mixture of disbelief and nervous dismissal. In 1924, reports reached the Gulf that cultured pearls were being detected in the markets of Bahrain and India. Merchants scoffed, confident that the discerning eye could always tell the difference, and that the allure of a natural gem, wrested from the sea by human effort, could never be replaced by a factory product. A British trade report from 1909 had confidently predicted that "It does not appear probable that the artificial pearl, however well made, will ever take the place of the natural one." This proved to be a catastrophic miscalculation.

The cultured pearl was a classic disruptive technology. It offered a product of consistent quality and appearance at a fraction of the cost. A process that in nature required a diver to risk his life for one lucky find among a hundred oysters could now be achieved with an almost 80 percent success rate on a farm. The mystique of the natural pearl could not compete with the simple economics of mass production. The new pearls began to flood the luxury markets of Europe and America, undermining the price of the Gulf's natural harvest. The traditional pearling industry, with its massive overheads of boats, crews, and provisions, and its reliance on a debt-based system, was simply unable to compete.

Just as this technological tsunami was hitting the industry, a second, even greater, wave struck from the West. On October 29, 1929, the American stock market crashed, triggering the Great Depression. The economic contagion spread rapidly across the globe, wiping out fortunes, shuttering industries, and throwing millions out of work. In an instant, the global market for luxury goods evaporated. Diamonds, fine furs, and, of course, pearls became unsellable extravagances in a world preoccupied with bread lines and soup kitchens. Demand for Gulf pearls, already weakened by the cultured pearl, now collapsed completely. Prices for natural pearls, which had already been falling, plummeted. Pearl exports from the Gulf fell to between 30 and 50 percent of their value in the 1920s. The two-punch combination of the cultured pearl and the Great Depression was fatal.

For Qatar, the result was an economic and social catastrophe of unimaginable proportions. The collapse of the pearling industry was not like a factory closing; it was as if the very ground beneath the country had dissolved. The entire economic structure, which had sustained the peninsula for centuries, disintegrated in the space of a few years. The dhows that once set sail with fanfare each summer now lay idle and rotting on the shores. The bustling souqs fell silent. The complex social hierarchy of wealthy merchants, boat captains (*nakhudas*), divers, and haulers became meaningless overnight.

The human cost was immense. With no income from the sea, widespread poverty, hunger, and malnutrition became rampant. Families were forced to sell their possessions, including the very pearl jewelry that had once been their pride, simply to buy food. Society was turned upside down. The system of debt that had indentured generations of divers to their captains became irrelevant when there was no catch to measure against the loans. Captains and divers, rich and poor, were suddenly thrust into the same desperate predicament. The period became known throughout the Gulf as the "Years of Hunger."

The demographic impact was stark. With no prospects at home, a great migration began. Thousands of Qataris were forced to leave their homeland in search of survival. Some moved inland, abandoning the coast to attempt subsistence farming in the harsh desert, while many others left the peninsula altogether. They sought work in the newly developing oil fields of Bahrain, Saudi Arabia, and Kuwait, or took jobs as laborers in the larger, more diversified cities of the Gulf. The population of Qatar, estimated at around 27,000 in 1908, plummeted. One estimate suggests that by 1949, after years of hardship, the population had dwindled to only

16,000. The coastal villages, once the vibrant heart of the nation, were hollowed out, some abandoned entirely.

For the ruler, Sheikh Abdullah bin Jassim Al Thani, the crisis was the greatest test of his leadership. The collapse of the pearl trade had not only impoverished his people; it had bankrupted his state. His main source of revenue, the taxes on pearling boats and their catch, had vanished. He was now the leader of a destitute nation, struggling to feed its people and maintain a basic semblance of order. The crisis was compounded in 1937 when Bahrain, in a dispute over sovereignty claims, declared a trade and travel embargo on the peninsula, further isolating the struggling sheikhdom.

Deeply in debt and in desperate need of cash, Sheikh Abdullah was forced to seek any possible alternative. The only glimmer of hope on the horizon was a new commodity that was beginning to transform the fortunes of his neighbors: oil. As early as 1922, representatives of the Anglo-Persian Oil Company (APOC) had sought an exploratory lease, and a preliminary survey was conducted in 1926. At the time, with pearling still viable, the terms were not sufficiently attractive. By the early 1930s, however, the situation had changed dramatically. The discovery of oil in Bahrain in 1932 made the geology of the surrounding region, including Qatar, a subject of intense interest.

The crippling poverty of his country gave Sheikh Abdullah very little leverage in negotiations with the powerful British oil companies. He knew, however, that a concession was his only path to salvation. His primary concern, beyond any financial remuneration, was security. In exchange for granting exclusive rights to explore for oil, he insisted that the British government upgrade the 1916 treaty to include a guarantee of protection against attacks by land, not just by sea. After lengthy and difficult negotiations, the British, keen to secure the concession for a British company, finally agreed.

On May 17, 1935, Sheikh Abdullah signed a 75-year oil concession with representatives of APOC, covering the entire territory of Qatar. In return, he received an immediate payment of 400,000 rupees and the promise of an annual payment of 150,000 rupees, a lifeline for his bankrupt government. More importantly, he received the enhanced treaty of protection he had sought.

The signing of the oil concession marked the definitive end of one era and the tentative beginning of another. The people of Qatar, still mired in the worst economic depression in their history, did not know it yet. For them, life remained a daily struggle for survival. The pearling industry would linger on for a few more years, a ghost of its former self, with a few boats still going out for meager profits, but its reign was over. The future of the peninsula no longer lay in the shallow waters of the Gulf, but deep beneath the desert rock. The calamitous collapse of the pearl trade had brought Qatar to its knees, but in its desperation, it had been forced to open the door to a new and unimaginably different destiny.

CHAPTER ELEVEN: The Dawn of the Oil Age: The First Concessions and Discoveries

The signing of the oil concession on May 17, 1935, was an act of profound desperation and faint hope. For Sheikh Abdullah bin Jassim Al Thani, the immediate influx of 400,000 rupees was a lifeline, a sum to keep his impoverished statelet from complete collapse. For the people of Qatar, mired in the bleakest years of the post-pearling depression, the arcane legalisms of an agreement signed with foreign men in suits meant little. Life remained a grinding struggle for survival. Yet, that document represented the country's last gamble, a bet on a hidden resource that geologists suspected, but could not guarantee, lay beneath the peninsula's barren rock.

The concession had been granted to the Anglo-Persian Oil Company (APOC), the British petroleum giant. However, due to the complex and cartel-like "Red Line Agreement" that governed the operations of the major Western oil companies in the former Ottoman Empire, APOC could not operate in Qatar alone. To manage the concession, it created a new subsidiary company, Petroleum Development (Qatar) Ltd., or PDQ, in 1937. The ownership of this new entity was a consortium of the titans of the global oil industry: APOC (later British Petroleum), Royal Dutch Shell, a French company, and two American firms, with a small remaining share held by the Armenian magnate Calouste Gulbenkian. Qatar's future was now in the hands of a multinational enterprise whose resources and global reach were beyond anything the peninsula had ever encountered.

In the winter of 1937, the first teams of geologists arrived to begin the painstaking work of mapping the peninsula and identifying the most promising location for a test well. To these Westerners, Qatar was an alien landscape. It was a pre-industrial society with no paved roads, no electricity, and no deep-water port. The searing summer heat was a formidable obstacle, and fresh water was a scarce and precious commodity. The logistical challenges were immense. Everything required for a modern industrial operation, from drilling rigs and trucks to food and medical supplies, had to be shipped in, often from Bahrain, and laboriously brought ashore.

The geologists' attention was quickly drawn to a prominent geological feature on the western coast, a long, north-south running ridge of limestone known as the Dukhan anticline. An anticline is an arch-like fold in the rock strata, a structure known to be an excellent trap for oil and gas. Based on their surveys, a specific location was chosen for the first exploratory well. A small camp was established in the desolate landscape, a cluster of tents and temporary buildings that marked the first outpost of the new oil age. The contrast with the traditional Qatari way of life could not have been starker. Bedouin tribes, whose rhythms had been dictated by the seasons and the search for grazing, now watched with curiosity as heavy machinery rumbled across the desert and a strange new tower began to rise from the sand.

Drilling of the well, officially designated Dukhan No. 1, began in October 1938. The work was slow and arduous. The rig bored day and night through layers of rock, the crew battling the intense heat and the constant mechanical challenges. For over a year, the drill bit descended deeper into the earth with no guarantee of success. Sheikh Abdullah and his officials waited anxiously. The annual concession payments were keeping the government afloat, but the real prize, the royalty payment that would come with commercial production, remained an elusive dream.

Then, in the final weeks of 1939, the breakthrough came. The drill hit a porous layer of Upper Jurassic limestone, a geological formation similar to that of the prolific Dammam field discovered in Saudi Arabia a few years earlier. The well showed promising signs of oil. By January 1940, Dukhan No. 1 was completed at a depth of over 1,700 meters, and tests confirmed a flow rate of nearly 4,500 barrels of high-quality oil per day. After years of poverty and despair, the gamble had paid off. Qatar was officially an oil state.

The timing of this momentous discovery, however, could not have been worse. On September 1, 1939, just weeks before oil was struck, Germany had invaded Poland, plunging Europe into the Second World War. The Persian Gulf, a vital artery for Britain's empire and its primary source of oil, instantly became a region of high strategic importance. The priorities of the British government and the oil companies shifted overnight from commercial development to the war effort. The resources, steel, and manpower needed to develop a new oil field were urgently required elsewhere.

Despite the outbreak of war, PDQ drilled two more appraisal wells to determine the extent of the field. Dukhan No. 2 was drilled 16 kilometers to the south in March 1941, and Dukhan No. 3 was drilled five kilometers east of the discovery well in May 1942. Both wells also struck oil, confirming that the Dukhan field was a significant discovery. But with the war raging and the threat of Axis expansion looming, developing the field was impossible. In June 1942, the decision was made to suspend all operations. The three wells were plugged with cement, and the equipment and installations were dismantled or, in some cases, destroyed to prevent them from falling into enemy hands. The small contingent of foreign oil workers packed up and left. The promise of oil wealth, so tantalizingly close, was put on indefinite hold.

For Qatar, the war years were a period of suspended animation. The country returned to its state of quiet poverty, the skeletal remains of the drilling rigs at Dukhan the only sign of the future that had been deferred. The annual concession payments from PDQ continued, a meager but essential source of income for Sheikh Abdullah's administration, but they did little to change the daily lives of his people. The world was aflame, and the small, isolated protectorate could do little but wait for the storm to pass.

It was not until the end of 1947, more than two years after the end of the war, that the oil men returned and operations at Dukhan resumed. The task facing them was enormous. They had to rebuild the camps, bring in new equipment, and recruit a workforce. The immediate priority was to develop the Dukhan field for full-scale commercial production. Over the next three years, an intense campaign of drilling began, with multiple rigs working continuously to prepare the field for exploitation.

The greatest challenge, however, was not getting the oil out of the ground, but getting it to market. The Dukhan field was on the remote western coast of the peninsula, far from any natural deep-water harbors. A major feat of engineering was required. The plan was to build a pipeline stretching clear across the width of Qatar to a suitable point on the more sheltered eastern coast from which tankers could be loaded.

The site chosen for the new oil terminal was a desolate spot on the southeast coast called Mesaieed, also known as Umm Said. Its deep-water access made it an ideal location. Beginning in 1949, this uninhabited stretch of coastline was transformed into the nerve center of Qatar's new industry. A 120-kilometer pipeline was constructed to connect the Dukhan field to the new terminal. At Mesaieed, huge storage tanks were erected to hold the crude oil, along with pumping stations and sea-loading lines that extended out into the Gulf. It was the first major industrial construction project in the country's history, requiring vast amounts of labor and materials.

Finally, by the end of 1949, after a decade of discovery, delay, and development, all the pieces were in place. The wells were ready, the pipeline was complete, and the terminal at Mesaieed was operational. On December 31, 1949, the tanker S.S. *President Manny* tied up at the new terminal and began to take on Qatar's first-ever shipment of crude oil. The 80,000-ton cargo was bound for Europe. After a long and painful decade of waiting, the dawn of Qatar's oil age had finally, truly arrived.

CHAPTER TWELVE: Post-War Boom: The Transformation of Qatari Society

The departure of the S.S. *President Manny* on the last day of 1949, its holds filled with Qatar's first crude oil export, was more than a commercial transaction; it was the closing of a door on one historical reality and the opening of another. The decade of abject poverty that followed the collapse of the pearl industry was over. The era of waiting, which had stretched through the long years of the Second World War, had ended. For a nation that had dwindled to a population of perhaps 16,000 souls, subsisting in a handful of sun-baked coastal towns, the torrent of wealth about to be unleashed was utterly transformative. It would remake the physical landscape, reshape the very structure of society, and redefine what it meant to be Qatari in the space of a single generation.

The scale of the change was staggering. In 1950, Qatar's oil revenue was a modest but significant $1 million. By 1954, that figure had skyrocketed to $23 million. This exponential growth was fueled by a renegotiated concession agreement in 1952, which established a 50-50 profit-sharing arrangement between the government and the oil company, bringing Qatar in line with other producers in the region. The money that flowed into the state's coffers was unlike anything the Al Thani rulers had ever commanded. It was a river of gold that made the revenues from the most prosperous pearling season in history look like a dried-up wadi.

The man tasked with managing this new reality was Sheikh Ali bin Abdullah Al Thani. Just a few months before the first oil shipment, in August 1949, his elderly father, Sheikh Abdullah bin Jassim, had formally abdicated in his favor. Sheikh Abdullah, the patient leader who had secured the British treaty and the oil concession, retired from public life, having guided his country to the very brink of its new destiny. Sheikh Ali, born in 1895, inherited a country with no formal government apparatus, no modern infrastructure, and a people with urgent, unmet needs. His reign, from 1949 to 1960, would be dedicated to the foundational task of building a modern state from the ground up.

The project of modernization was all-encompassing, a headlong rush to build in a decade what other nations had developed over centuries. The first priority was to create the basic sinews of a functional country. Doha, still a cluster of traditional courtyard houses made from mud and coral, began its transformation. A new road network was planned, a proper airstrip was constructed to replace the old one, and a deep-water port was dredged to allow larger ships to dock, ending the laborious process of offloading cargo onto smaller boats. In 1953, the country's first telephone exchange opened, connecting Qatar to the outside world as never before. A year later, the first water desalination plant was commissioned, a crucial step in overcoming the peninsula's chronic lack of fresh water. This was soon followed by a power generation station, which for the first time brought electricity to the homes of citizens, often free of charge.

Parallel to this physical construction was the creation of a social welfare state, funded entirely by oil revenues. Two areas received immediate and profound investment: healthcare and education. Before the oil boom, healthcare was rudimentary, a mix of traditional remedies and a small, 12-bed hospital established with the help of the American Mission in the 1940s. With the new wealth, Sheikh Ali's government commissioned a proper state hospital. In 1952, the Royal Institute of British Architects held a competition for the design, and in 1957, the Al Rumailah Hospital opened its doors. It was the first modern, well-equipped medical facility in the country's history, a tangible symbol of the state's new commitment to the well-being of its citizens.

The transformation in education was equally dramatic. For centuries, education had been the preserve of the *kuttab*, small Quranic schools that taught basic literacy and religious principles. In 1949, the first formal school for boys, Islah al-Mohammadiyeh, was established with just 50 students. By 1954, there were four schools with over 500 students. The government began a concerted effort to build a national school system, often having to import teachers from other Arab countries like Egypt and Palestine. In a profoundly significant step, the first formal school for girls was opened in 1955, and by 1957, girls' education was officially integrated into the national system under the newly founded Ministry of Education. The state not only provided education for free but also offered incentives to encourage families, many of whom were skeptical of secular schooling, to send their children to the new institutions.

This whirlwind of development created an insatiable demand for labor, a demand that the tiny native Qatari population could not possibly meet. The result was a demographic explosion. Qatar, which had seen its population shrink during the pearling collapse, now became a magnet for migrants from across the world. Tens of thousands of workers arrived: Palestinians, Egyptians, and Yemenis from the Arab world; Iranians from across the Gulf; Pakistanis and Indians from the subcontinent; and a new class of Western engineers, managers, and advisers, mostly British, who were essential for building and running the new oil industry and government departments. The population, estimated at around 25,000 in 1950, grew exponentially. By 1960, it had more than doubled to over 47,000, and by 1970, it would reach 111,000. For the first time in its history, the native Qatari population became a minority in its own country, a demographic reality that would shape its social and political landscape for decades to come.

This influx of people accelerated the process of urbanization. The old pearling villages began to empty out as families moved to the capital, drawn by the prospect of jobs, housing, and access to the new schools and clinics. Doha was no longer a quiet coastal town; it was a sprawling construction site. Traditional life, organized around the tribe and the sea, began to give way to a new urban existence based on wage labor and government employment. Qataris who had once been divers or fishermen now became policemen, clerks, and drivers. The government became the primary employer, and a Qatari citizen's relationship with the state was redefined. The ruler was no longer just a tribal sheikh to whom one owed allegiance; he was the head of a paternalistic system that provided a salary, a house, free water and electricity, and healthcare from cradle to grave.

Administering this new and complex society required a government. Under the tutelage of British advisers, the rudimentary beginnings of a modern bureaucracy were established. In 1949, the first British political agent took up residence in Doha, formalizing the relationship of protection and advice. A modern police force was established in 1949 to maintain security in a rapidly growing and diverse society. Gradually, fledgling departments were created to oversee key areas like education, health, public works, and finance. A British adviser was brought in to create the state's first-ever formal budget in 1953. These nascent institutions were often staffed by a mix of Al Thani family members, trusted local merchants, and foreign experts. A key figure in this period was the ruler's grandson, Khalifa bin Hamad Al Thani, who as a young man was appointed to several key posts, including director of education and chief of security forces, gaining valuable experience that would shape his own future rule.

The transition was not without its tensions. The sudden, astronomical wealth created internal pressures within the ruling family over the distribution of revenues. Sheikh Ali's reputation for piety and generosity was tested by the demands of his relatives. The rapid influx of foreigners created new social dynamics and occasional friction. For the older generation of Qataris, the pace of change was bewildering. A man who had spent his youth diving for pearls from a wooden dhow now saw his sons driving American cars on paved roads and listening to radios broadcasting news from Cairo and London. The very fabric of society—the patriarchal authority of elders, the strict separation of roles, the isolation from the outside world—was being rewoven at bewildering speed. There were protests and labor strikes among oil workers in the mid-1950s, influenced by the rising tide of Arab nationalism sweeping the region, which gave the ruler cause for concern.

By 1960, as his decade of rule drew to a close, Sheikh Ali bin Abdullah Al Thani presided over a country that was physically and socially unrecognizable from the one he had inherited. The foundations of a modern welfare state had been laid, and the path towards an oil-fueled future was firmly set. On October 24, 1960, citing a desire to retire, he abdicated in favor of his son, Ahmad bin Ali Al Thani. He left behind a country still grappling with the immense challenges of its sudden transformation, but one that had been decisively pulled from the poverty of its past and set on a trajectory of almost unimaginable prosperity.

CHAPTER THIRTEEN: The Road to Independence: The 1960s and British Withdrawal

The abdication of Sheikh Ali bin Abdullah Al Thani on October 24, 1960, passed the leadership of Qatar to his son, Sheikh Ahmad bin Ali Al Thani. Born in 1922, Sheikh Ahmad ascended to the throne of a country in the throes of a bewilderingly rapid transformation. The foundations of a modern state had been laid in the 1950s, but the structure was far from complete. The new ruler, however, was a man whose passions lay elsewhere. An affable and generous figure, Sheikh Ahmad was renowned for his love of falconry and hunting, pursuits that frequently took him abroad for extended periods, particularly to his villa in Switzerland. While he was the undisputed sovereign, the vital, day-to-day task of governing and continuing the arduous process of state-building fell to his younger cousin and designated heir apparent, Sheikh Khalifa bin Hamad Al Thani.

This arrangement created a unique dual power structure that would define Qatar throughout the decade. Sheikh Ahmad was the head of state, the ultimate authority to whom allegiance was sworn. Sheikh Khalifa, appointed Deputy Ruler and Heir Apparent on the day of Sheikh Ahmad's accession, was the de facto head of government, the tireless administrator who held the reins of the burgeoning bureaucracy. Sheikh Khalifa, a grandson of the formidable Sheikh Abdullah bin Jassim, had been immersed in the mechanics of governance from a young age, serving as chief of the security forces and director of education. He was a modernist and a pragmatist, keenly aware that the torrent of oil wealth, if not managed with discipline and foresight, could be squandered.

One of Sheikh Khalifa's first and most urgent priorities was to bring order to the state's chaotic finances. In the early years of the oil boom, revenues were treated as the personal income of the ruler, who then distributed them among the sprawling Al Thani family and funded development projects as he saw fit. While this was in keeping with traditional patriarchal rule, it was wildly inadequate for the needs of a modern state. Extravagant spending by some senior members of the ruling family was draining a significant portion of the country's income. To counter this, Sheikh Khalifa worked to create a formal government budget, a revolutionary concept for the time. This was a direct challenge to the old way of doing things, an attempt to separate the finances of the state from the private purse of the ruler and his relatives. His efforts were met with resistance, but he persevered, understanding that fiscal discipline was the bedrock of a stable state.

Throughout the 1960s, under Sheikh Khalifa's steady hand, the machinery of a modern state was assembled piece by piece. Government departments, which had been rudimentary bodies in the 1950s, were expanded and given greater authority. A proper civil service began to take shape. The legal system was overhauled with the establishment of the country's first secular courts, which operated alongside the traditional Sharia courts. In 1961, a crucial step towards economic sovereignty was taken with the creation of the Qatar and Dubai Currency Board. This new body issued a common currency, the Qatar and Dubai riyal, to replace the Indian external rupee, which had long been the standard medium of exchange in the lower Gulf. This move shielded the local economy from the fluctuations of Indian monetary policy and was a clear assertion of a separate economic identity.

The physical transformation of the country also continued apace. The capital, Doha, was the focus of intense development, with new housing projects, government buildings, and commercial districts replacing the old fabric of the town. In 1964, the government established the country's first national cement company, a strategic investment to ensure a local supply for the endless construction. The Khalifa Sports City was inaugurated, signaling a new interest in national recreation. The state's welfare system, providing free healthcare, education, housing, water, and electricity, was expanded, embedding a social contract between the ruling family and the citizenry that was entirely underwritten by oil revenues.

While Qatar was consumed with its internal development, the wider political landscape of the Middle East was seething. The potent ideology of Arab nationalism, championed by Egypt's charismatic president, Gamal Abdel Nasser, swept across the region. Nasser's message of pan-Arab unity, anti-imperialism, and republicanism resonated deeply, particularly among the educated and politically aware youth in the Gulf. This created an atmosphere of unease for the traditional monarchies of the peninsula, with their deep-seated treaty relationships with Great Britain. The British, long seen as the ultimate guarantors of security, were increasingly portrayed by nationalist voices as colonial overlords propping up anachronistic regimes.

For the British themselves, the world had changed irrevocably since the end of the Second World War. The Suez Crisis of 1956 had been a humiliating blow to British prestige in the region. Decolonization was sweeping through Africa and Asia, and the economic cost of maintaining a global military presence was becoming unsustainable. By the mid-1960s, the British economy was in serious trouble, facing a persistent balance of payments crisis and the devaluation of the pound sterling. The government of Prime Minister Harold Wilson was forced to make drastic cuts to public spending. The days of Britain policing the world were coming to an end.

The announcement, when it came, was nevertheless a bombshell. On January 16, 1968, the British government declared its intention to withdraw all its military forces from the Persian Gulf and the Far East by the end of 1971. For the rulers of the Gulf, from Kuwait to the shores of Oman, the news was a profound shock. For more than 150 years, the security of the region had been underpinned by British naval power and a web of treaties. The Pax Britannica had suppressed piracy, deterred regional predators, and allowed the small coastal sheikhdoms to develop without the constant fear of invasion. Now, suddenly, the ultimate protector was leaving.

The British departure created an urgent power vacuum. The rulers of the nine sheikhdoms directly affected—Bahrain, Qatar, and the seven Trucial States (Abu Dhabi, Dubai, Sharjah, Ajman, Umm Al Quwain, Ras Al Khaimah, and Fujairah)—were faced with an existential challenge. Individually, they were small, wealthy, and vulnerable. The Shah of Iran harbored a long-standing territorial claim to Bahrain, Saudi Arabia had its own ambitions, and Iraq periodically renewed its claim to Kuwait. The prospect of instability and conflict was very real.

Britain's proposed solution, strongly encouraged by its diplomats, was for the nine sheikhdoms to band together and form a single, unified state. The idea had a certain logic. A federation would be able to pool its resources to create a credible defense force, speak with a unified voice in international affairs, and provide a more stable political framework than a collection of tiny, rivalrous statelets. The idea was immediately taken up by two of the most influential rulers in the region: the visionary Sheikh Zayed bin Sultan Al Nahyan of Abu Dhabi and the pragmatic Sheikh Rashid bin Saeed Al Maktoum of Dubai. In February 1968, just a month after the British announcement, they met and agreed in principle to form a union, inviting the other seven rulers to join them.

Thus began nearly three years of intense, complex, and often fraught negotiations to create the Federation of Arab Emirates. Sheikh Khalifa bin Hamad, representing Qatar, plunged into the discussions with determination. He was a firm believer in the ideal of unity and saw a strong federation as the best guarantee of Qatar's future security. The Supreme Council of the nine rulers began to meet regularly, and committees were established to hammer out the details of a federal constitution. The initial optimism, however, soon collided with the hard realities of local politics and rival interests.

Several major sticking points emerged. The first was the question of representation. Bahrain, with the largest native population, argued for representation based on population size. Qatar, with its immense wealth but smaller population, feared being marginalized in such a system and favored the principle of the sovereign equality of all member states. The smaller, poorer Trucial States worried about being dominated by their larger, wealthier neighbors. The second major issue was the location of a federal capital. Several locations were proposed, but no consensus could be reached.

Deeper disagreements revolved around the very nature of the federation. Sheikh Zayed of Abu Dhabi, flush with new oil revenues, advocated for a strong, centralized federal government with significant powers over defense, foreign policy, and the budget. He was willing to contribute generously to fund such a state. Sheikh Khalifa of Qatar largely supported this vision. Sheikh Rashid of Dubai, however, whose emirate thrived on its status as a freewheeling commercial entrepôt, was wary of ceding too much authority to a central government, particularly in matters of customs and trade.

As the negotiations dragged on, Qatar and Bahrain, the two most advanced states in terms of their administrative and institutional development, grew increasingly frustrated with the slower pace and internal disputes of the Trucial States. By 1970, it was becoming clear that the vision of a nine-state federation was foundering on these intractable disagreements.

The final unraveling of the grand federation plan was precipitated by two key developments. The first was a shift in Iranian policy. In March 1970, the Shah of Iran, under diplomatic pressure from Britain and the United States, agreed to drop his country's long-standing territorial claim to Bahrain, subject to a United Nations survey of the island's population to ascertain their wishes. The UN mission quickly confirmed that the overwhelming majority of Bahrainis favored independence. With the threat of Iranian annexation removed, Bahrain's primary incentive for joining the federation evaporated. It could now confidently pursue a future as a sovereign state.

With Bahrain's intentions becoming clear, and the constitutional talks still deadlocked, Sheikh Khalifa concluded that Qatar's interests would be best served by following a similar path. The prospect of being yoked to the less developed Trucial States in a federation without Bahrain was not an appealing one. The time had come for Qatar to prepare for its own independence.

The process was swift and decisive. On April 2, 1970, Sheikh Ahmad bin Ali Al Thani promulgated Qatar's Provisional Constitution, a landmark document that had been drafted under Sheikh Khalifa's direction. It was the country's first formal constitution, outlining a framework for governance based on an executive Council of Ministers, an advisory legislative council, and an independent judiciary. It declared Qatar an independent, sovereign Arab state with Islam as its official religion.

The next logical step followed on May 28, 1970, with the formation of Qatar's first-ever Council of Ministers. The cabinet was a blend of Al Thani family members and prominent commoners. Crucially, Sheikh Khalifa bin Hamad Al Thani, already the Deputy Ruler and Heir Apparent, was formally appointed as the nation's first Prime Minister, cementing his position as the central figure in the country's governance.

Over the next year, Sheikh Khalifa's government worked to establish the final institutions of statehood and negotiate the end of the 1916 treaty with Britain. This culminated in the signing of a new Treaty of Friendship between the two countries, one that replaced the old protectorate relationship with one based on mutual respect between sovereign equals. With all the legal and constitutional preparations complete, the moment had arrived.

On the morning of September 3, 1971, the people of Qatar gathered around their radios to hear a historic announcement. A government spokesman, in a voice filled with gravity, read the official proclamation of independence. The 1916 treaty with Great Britain was terminated. Qatar was now a fully independent and sovereign state. The British flag was lowered from the agency building in Doha for the final time. A few weeks later, the new nation took its place on the world stage, joining both the Arab League and the United Nations. After decades of protection, years of frantic development, and a final, tense period of diplomatic maneuvering, the road to independence had reached its destination.

CHAPTER FOURTEEN: Statehood and the Early Years of Independence: 1971-1980

The proclamation of independence on September 3, 1971, was a moment of profound and quiet significance. There were no mass rallies in the streets of Doha, no revolutionary fervor, just a formal radio announcement that the long era of British protection was over. Qatar, a nation whose modern identity had been forged in the crucible of imperial rivalries and whose very existence had been secured by a foreign treaty, was now master of its own destiny. The challenges were formidable. The new state was small, its native population barely a fifth of the total number of residents, and its security in a volatile region was far from guaranteed. Its first steps onto the world stage were taken with a deliberate and measured pace. Within weeks, Qatar had joined the Arab League and was admitted as the 127th member of the United Nations, its new flag of white and maroon hoisted for the first time in New York. The work of building a nation, however, had only just begun.

While Sheikh Ahmad bin Ali Al Thani was the sovereign and head of state, the architect and driving force of the new government remained his cousin, the Prime Minister and Heir Apparent, Sheikh Khalifa bin Hamad Al Thani. For a decade, Sheikh Khalifa had been the de facto ruler, the tireless administrator who had assembled the machinery of a modern state. The dual power structure that had characterized the 1960s, with Sheikh Ahmad often absent for long hunting trips abroad, had become increasingly untenable in the face of the demands of full sovereignty. An independent state required a leader who was consistently present, one who could provide hands-on direction for the complex tasks of domestic development and international diplomacy. The situation was an open secret in the Gulf, a source of quiet concern among Qatar's neighbors and allies.

The resolution came just over five months after independence. On February 22, 1972, while Sheikh Ahmad was on a hunting trip in

Iran, Sheikh Khalifa, with the unanimous support of the Al Thani ruling family and the allegiance of the country's security forces, assumed the position of Emir. The transfer of power was swift, bloodless, and widely seen as a necessary step to ensure the stability and progress of the new state. In his first public address as Emir, Sheikh Khalifa framed the move not as a coup, but as a corrective measure to rectify a situation that was hampering the nation's development. He pledged to usher in a new era of reform, to modernize the government, and, most critically, to ensure that the country's burgeoning oil wealth was directed towards the public good rather than private enrichment.

Sheikh Khalifa moved quickly to make good on his promises. One of his first and most significant acts was to amend the 1970 Provisional Constitution. The amendments streamlined the government, abolishing the post of Deputy Ruler and strengthening the powers of the Emir and the Council of Ministers. A key reform was the creation of a new Ministry of Finance and Petroleum, a portfolio Sheikh Khalifa kept for himself, signaling his intention to personally oversee the nation's most vital resource. He also established an Advisory Council, or *Majlis al-Shura*, as stipulated in the constitution. Thirty members, initially all appointed, were tasked with debating legislation and advising the government, a first, cautious step towards public participation in the political process.

A central plank of his reform program was tackling the thorny issue of ruling family allowances. Under the previous arrangement, a substantial portion of the state's oil revenue— estimated by some at between a quarter and a half—was allocated directly to the ruler and other senior sheikhs. This practice, a legacy of the patriarchal system where state and personal funds were intertwined, was a massive drain on the national treasury. Sheikh Khalifa, determined to fund his ambitious development plans, took the politically sensitive step of dramatically cutting these allowances and redirecting the funds into the state budget. The message was clear: the era of profligacy was over, and the oil wealth belonged to the nation as a whole.

This assertion of national control over the country's finances was mirrored by an even more significant move: the nationalization of the oil and gas industry. When Qatar became independent, its entire hydrocarbon sector was still owned and operated by a consortium of foreign oil companies, principally the Qatar Petroleum Company (QPC) on land and the Shell Company of Qatar (SCQ) offshore. These companies paid royalties and taxes to the state, but the ultimate decisions about production levels, investment, and marketing remained in foreign hands. For the newly independent state, this was a galling symbol of economic dependency. Sheikh Khalifa, echoing a sentiment that was sweeping across the oil-producing world, believed that true sovereignty was impossible without direct control over the nation's primary resource.

The opportunity to change this dynamic arrived with the geopolitical earthquake of the October 1973 Arab-Israeli War. In response to Western support for Israel, the Arab members of the Organization of Petroleum Exporting Countries (OPEC), including Qatar, decided to wield the "oil weapon." They announced a coordinated cut in production and, most critically, imposed a total embargo on oil shipments to the United States and other nations deemed hostile. The effect on the global economy was immediate and profound. Panic buying on the spot markets sent prices skyrocketing. In a matter of months, the price of a barrel of oil quadrupled, rising from around $3 to over $12.

For Qatar, the 1973 oil crisis was a revolutionary event. Overnight, the state's revenues were quadrupled, unleashing a tsunami of wealth that dwarfed even the initial boom of the 1950s. This unprecedented financial windfall gave Sheikh Khalifa the leverage he needed to accelerate the takeover of the oil industry. The process was methodical and staged. In 1973, the government took an initial 25 percent stake in the foreign oil companies. By early 1974, buoyed by the new price reality, this was increased to a 60 percent controlling share. The final step was inevitable. In July 1974, Sheikh Khalifa issued a decree establishing the Qatar General Petroleum Corporation (QGPC), a new national entity tasked with overseeing all phases of the country's oil and gas industry. Over the next two years, QGPC negotiated the final takeover, and by late 1976, the state had acquired 100 percent ownership of both QPC and SCQ. After four decades, Qatar's oil was finally its own.

The sheer scale of the new revenues was almost impossible to comprehend. The state budget, which stood at a respectable 200 million Qatari riyals in 1970, exploded to 1.3 billion in 1974 and would reach an astonishing 19 billion by the end of the decade. This deluge of petrodollars fueled a second, even more intense, wave of national development. If the 1950s had been about building the basic infrastructure of a state, the 1970s were about building an industrial nation. Sheikh Khalifa's vision was to use the finite wealth generated from extracting raw materials to create a diversified, modern economy that could sustain the country long after the oil wells ran dry.

The focal point of this industrial ambition was the coastal area of Umm Said, which was rapidly transformed from a simple oil terminal into a sprawling industrial city. It became home to a series of massive, capital-intensive projects, typically established as joint ventures with experienced foreign partners who could provide the necessary technology and expertise. The first of these landmark enterprises was the Qatar Fertiliser Company (QAFCO), which had begun production in 1973, using the country's abundant natural gas as a feedstock to produce ammonia and urea for the global agricultural market.

This was quickly followed by a series of other foundational industries. In 1974, construction began on a steel mill, the Qatar Steel Company (QASCO), a joint venture with Japanese partners. It was the first integrated steel plant in the Gulf, a project of immense national pride that began production in 1978. That same year, the Qatar Petrochemical Company (QAPCO) was established in partnership with a French firm to produce ethylene and polyethylene, leveraging the gas resources that were a by-product of oil extraction. Power generation and water desalination capacity were massively expanded to fuel these new industries and the rapidly growing population. The state, through QGPC, was investing its oil profits on a colossal scale, betting that it could transform gas and capital into steel, plastics, and fertilizers.

This industrialization drive was accompanied by a commensurate boom in civil infrastructure. Doha's transformation, which had begun in the 1950s, accelerated dramatically. A new international airport was built to accommodate jumbo jets, and the deep-water port was expanded. A modern ring-road system was laid down to ease the city's chronic traffic congestion, caused by a sudden explosion in the number of cars on the road. Lavish new government ministries, a testament to the growing power of the state bureaucracy, rose alongside new hotels, like the Gulf Hotel, which became a landmark on the capital's shoreline. The state's welfare system was also supercharged. The government embarked on a massive program of building public housing, providing modern, subsidized homes to thousands of Qatari families, often replacing the traditional dwellings they had occupied for generations.

Alongside the construction of a modern economy, Sheikh Khalifa's government also invested heavily in the creation of a modern national identity. The goal was to foster a sense of shared citizenship that could unite the disparate tribes and provide a cultural anchor in a sea of rapid change. Two projects from this era stand out as particularly symbolic. The first was the Qatar National Museum, which opened in 1975. Housed in the beautifully restored Fariq Al-Salatah Palace, the former residence of Sheikh Abdullah bin Jassim, the museum was a deliberate and powerful statement. Instead of tearing down the old to make way for the new, the state had chosen its most prominent historical building as the vessel for its national story. The museum brilliantly showcased the country's history, from its pearling past and desert heritage to the story of the oil discovery, grounding the new, wealthy nation in a rich and authentic local history.

The second landmark institution was the University of Qatar. Founded in 1977 from the nucleus of two earlier colleges of education, the university was the apex of the country's new educational system. For the first time, young Qataris, both men and women, could pursue higher education in their own country. The university was conceived not just as a place of learning, but as a crucible for a new generation of Qatari technocrats, teachers, and leaders who would guide the nation's future. The state also dramatically expanded its scholarship program, sending thousands of students abroad to the finest universities in Europe, the United States, and the Arab world, with the expectation that they would return with the skills needed to run the increasingly complex machinery of a modern petro-state.

Qatar's foreign policy during this first decade of independence was characterized by caution and a firm commitment to regional consensus. Sheikh Khalifa worked to build solid relationships with his immediate neighbors, particularly Saudi Arabia, whose political and cultural weight made it the undisputed leader of the Arabian Peninsula. He signed a formal border agreement with the Kingdom in 1974, settling a long-standing issue. He also pursued a policy of active engagement with the wider Arab world, contributing generously to the "frontline states" bordering Israel and participating actively in pan-Arab organizations. Qatar established embassies and cultivated diplomatic ties, building the architecture of a foreign service from scratch.

As the decade drew to a close, however, the regional landscape began to shift in ways that would present new and dangerous challenges. In 1979, the Iranian Revolution overthrew the Shah, a fellow Gulf monarch, and replaced his pro-Western regime with a radical Islamic Republic. The new government in Tehran, with its revolutionary ideology, was viewed with deep suspicion and alarm by the conservative monarchies on the Arab side of the Gulf. The seizure of the Grand Mosque in Mecca by religious extremists that same year, followed swiftly by the Soviet invasion of Afghanistan, added to a growing sense of regional instability. The certainties of the 1970s, a decade defined by the exhilarating and all-consuming project of nation-building, were giving way to a new and more perilous era. Qatar, now a wealthy and established state, would have to navigate a region where the old rules no longer seemed to apply.

CHAPTER FIFTEEN: Navigating Regional Politics: The Iran-Iraq War and the GCC

The dawn of the 1980s found Qatar in an unfamiliar and somewhat unsettling position. The preceding decade had been a whirlwind of nation-building, a period of exhilarating, internally focused development fueled by the 1973 oil boom. Under the firm hand of Sheikh Khalifa bin Hamad Al Thani, the state had taken full control of its hydrocarbon resources and plowed the resulting revenues into creating the physical and social infrastructure of a modern country. The national mood was one of confident progress. But as the decade turned, the gaze of Qatar's leadership was forced outward, toward a regional landscape that was darkening with alarming speed. The 1979 Iranian Revolution had not only toppled a fellow monarch but had installed a radical, theocratic regime with an explicit policy of exporting its revolutionary ideals. The seizure of the Grand Mosque in Mecca and the Soviet invasion of Afghanistan that same year further shattered the old certainties. The comfortable, predictable security environment of the 1970s was gone, replaced by a new era of ideological conflict and military threat.

This new reality exploded into open warfare on September 22, 1980, when the armed forces of Saddam Hussein's Iraq crossed the border into Iran. The Iraqi leader, hoping for a swift victory that would make him the undisputed strongman of the Gulf, had badly miscalculated. The Iranian response was ferocious, and what was intended as a blitzkrieg rapidly bogged down into a brutal war of attrition that would last for eight agonizing years. For Qatar and the other small, fabulously wealthy Arab monarchies of the lower Gulf, the war on their doorstep was an existential crisis. They were geographically and demographically dwarfed by the two belligerents. Their entire economic model, based on the uninterrupted export of oil and gas through the narrow Strait of Hormuz, was suddenly vulnerable. The conflict was not a distant affair; its front lines were just a few hundred kilometers across the water, a constant, menacing presence.

Qatar's official position was one of Arab solidarity with Iraq. Along with the other Gulf monarchies, it viewed the new revolutionary government in Tehran as the primary threat to regional stability. An Iranian victory, it was feared, could destabilize their own societies and upend the conservative political order. This support, however, was carefully calibrated. While Saudi Arabia and Kuwait became the primary financial backers of the Iraqi war effort, providing tens of billions of dollars in loans and grants, Qatar's contribution was more modest and less overt. Reports from the time indicated that Qatar was among the Gulf states that lent money to Baghdad, but its support was deliberately muted. Sheikh Khalifa's government pursued a delicate balancing act, a policy of quiet pragmatism dictated by geography and demography.

This cautious approach was rooted in two fundamental realities. First, Iran was not a distant adversary but a powerful, permanent neighbor just across the Gulf. A policy of outright hostility was a luxury Qatar could not afford. The shared waters of the Gulf were a source of both wealth and vulnerability, and antagonizing Tehran could have severe consequences for Qatar's shipping and offshore installations. Second, Qatar, like other Gulf states, had a small but significant native Shia population. The government was keenly aware that an overly aggressive pro-Iraq stance could risk alienating this segment of its own citizenry. The policy, therefore, was to fulfill its obligations to the Arab consensus while strategically avoiding any action that might provoke direct Iranian retaliation. It was a tightrope walk that would define Qatari foreign policy for the entire decade.

The immediate and most tangible consequence of this new era of insecurity was a historic move toward collective defense. For years, the idea of a formal alliance among the Gulf monarchies had been discussed, but it took the twin shocks of the Iranian Revolution and the Iran-Iraq War to translate talk into action. On May 25, 1981, in Abu Dhabi, Sheikh Khalifa bin Hamad Al Thani joined the leaders of Saudi Arabia, Kuwait, Bahrain, the United Arab Emirates, and Oman to sign the charter establishing the

Cooperation Council for the Arab States of the Gulf, universally known as the Gulf Cooperation Council (GCC).

The creation of the GCC was a landmark event in the region's history and a cornerstone of Qatar's post-independence foreign policy. While the charter emphasized economic and social cooperation, its primary impetus was unquestionably security. It was an alliance of monarchies, a "club of kings," formed to protect the status quo in the face of revolutionary threats. For Qatar, the GCC provided a vital new framework for its security. The era of relying on a single, distant protector like Britain was over. The GCC offered a new doctrine of collective security, embedding Qatar in a regional alliance dominated by the political and military weight of Saudi Arabia. Qatar became a committed and active founding member, viewing the council as the essential first line of defense in a newly dangerous world.

Domestically, the 1980s were a period of consolidation and, compared to the frantic pace of the 1970s, relative austerity. The oil boom of the previous decade had given way to the oil glut of the 1980s. A global recession, increased energy conservation in the West, and new oil production from non-OPEC sources like the North Sea sent prices tumbling. Qatar's economy, almost entirely dependent on oil revenues, took a significant hit. Government spending was curtailed, and major development projects were delayed or scaled back. The decade was less about launching grand new industrial schemes and more about managing the ones already built. The focus shifted to improving efficiency at the industrial hub of Mesaieed, where the steel, fertilizer, and petrochemical plants established in the 1970s continued to be the centerpiece of the country's diversification strategy. The Industrial Development Technical Center, set up in 1981, played a key role in trying to organize and direct this next phase of industrialization.

Despite the economic headwinds, the state continued to expand its social welfare programs and build the institutions of a modern nation. Under Sheikh Khalifa's direction, the government focused on creating a legal and administrative framework to manage the country's development. Dozens of laws were issued to regulate everything from private schools to the establishment of the country's first tourism committee in 1980. This quiet, steady process of institutionalization was a hallmark of Sheikh Khalifa's rule, a deliberate effort to create a stable and predictable system of governance.

The ever-present backdrop to this domestic activity was the war raging to the north. As the conflict dragged on, it became increasingly dangerous for neutral shipping in the Gulf. In 1984, the conflict entered a new and perilous phase known as the "Tanker War." Iraq, unable to defeat Iran on the ground, began attacking Iranian oil terminals and tankers sailing from Kharg Island, hoping to cripple Iran's economy. Iran retaliated by attacking the ships of states that supported Iraq, primarily those sailing to and from Kuwait and Saudi Arabia.

For Qatar, this phase of the war was a direct threat. Its own tankers and LNG carriers had to navigate these newly dangerous waters. The risk of a stray missile or a mistaken attack was constant. In 1983, an Iraqi air raid on an Iranian offshore oil field threatened installations on the Qatari coast, forcing the government to hastily construct defensive barriers to protect its own facilities. The entire Gulf became a militarized zone. The navies of the United States, Britain, and other Western powers moved in to protect international shipping, particularly Kuwaiti tankers that were reflagged with the Stars and Stripes. The presence of these foreign navies provided a degree of security but also highlighted the region's vulnerability and dependence on outside powers. Qatar, which had previously opposed a superpower naval presence in the Gulf, now had little choice but to accept it as a necessary evil to keep the sea lanes open.

In response to these escalating threats, the GCC sought to bolster its own military capabilities. In 1984, the council formally established a joint military force, the Peninsula Shield Force, to be based in northeastern Saudi Arabia. Composed of troops from all six member states, its purpose was to act as a rapid intervention force to deter and respond to external aggression against any GCC member. Qatar contributed troops to the force and participated in its joint exercises, known as "Dir' Al Jazeera" (Peninsula Shield). While the force was too small to be a credible deterrent against a major power like Iran or Iraq, its creation was a symbolically important step, a physical manifestation of the principle that an attack on one member was an attack on all.

Throughout this period of heightened tension, Qatar continued its delicate diplomatic dance. Even while participating in GCC meetings that renewed support for Iraq, Sheikh Khalifa's government maintained what lines of communication it could with Iran. This quiet pragmatism paid dividends. In 1986, a territorial dispute flared up between Qatar and Bahrain over the Fasht al-Dibal shoals, a tiny but strategically located reef. In the ensuing standoff, Iran publicly sided with Qatar, a clear signal of appreciation for Doha's less confrontational stance during the war. It was a lesson in the complex, multi-layered politics of the Gulf, where an adversary in one context could be a useful friend in another. However, Qatar's loyalty to the GCC was never in doubt; when it came to Iran's dispute with the UAE over the islands of Abu Musa and the Greater and Lesser Tunbs, Qatar consistently backed its GCC partner.

When a UN-brokered ceasefire finally ended the Iran-Iraq War in August 1988, a collective sigh of relief was breathed across the Gulf. The immediate threat of the conflict spilling over had passed. But the eight-year war had fundamentally reshaped the strategic landscape. It had cost over a million lives and left both belligerents economically devastated. Iran remained a formidable, ideologically driven power, while Iraq had emerged from the war with a battle-hardened, million-man army and a mountain of debt owed to its Gulf neighbors. The GCC, and Qatar within it, had weathered its first great storm. The alliance had held together, providing a crucial framework for political and security cooperation. But the end of one conflict would soon reveal a new, and perhaps even more dangerous, threat. The regional order that emerged from the ashes of the Iran-Iraq War would prove to be fragile, and the assumptions that underpinned it would be shattered just two years later.

CHAPTER SIXTEEN: The North Field Discovery: The Gas Revolution Begins

In the mid-1980s, Qatar found itself in a precarious position. The exhilarating, state-building boom of the 1970s, fueled by the oil price shock of 1973, had given way to a sobering new reality. A global oil glut, driven by new production from the North Sea and elsewhere, had sent prices tumbling. Qatar's economy, which relied on its aging Dukhan oil field for more than 90 percent of government revenues, was contracting. The state budget was under pressure, and the era of limitless spending was over. The country's oil reserves were finite, projected to be largely depleted by 2023. For the government of Sheikh Khalifa bin Hamad Al Thani, the question of Qatar's long-term economic survival was no longer theoretical; it was an urgent, pressing concern. The answer, as it turned out, lay not in finding more oil, but in a colossal undersea reservoir of a different hydrocarbon, a resource that had been discovered years earlier and dismissed as a problem child.

The discovery itself had been almost accidental. In 1971, while drilling an exploratory well off the northeast coast, the Shell Company of Qatar stumbled upon an immense pocket of natural gas. It was not what they were looking for. In the energy landscape of the early 1970s, oil was king. Natural gas, particularly non-associated gas found in a field with no crude oil, was considered a liability. It was difficult and astronomically expensive to transport to markets, requiring either a multi-billion-dollar pipeline or a technologically complex and hazardous process of liquefaction. With oil cheap and plentiful, there was simply no market for Qatar's gas. Shell capped the well, and the discovery was shelved, an immense resource of little apparent value.

It took fourteen years and fifteen appraisal wells to begin to grasp the true scale of the find. The reservoir, which became known as the North Field, was not just large; it was the single largest non-associated natural gas field in the world. It was a geological freak, an enormous dome of gas-rich rock spanning an area roughly the size of Qatar itself, containing recoverable reserves of more than 900 trillion standard cubic feet—approximately 10 percent of the world's known supply. As the economic gloom of the 1980s descended, this once-unwanted discovery began to look less like a problem and more like a lifeline.

The decision to develop the North Field was the biggest and riskiest gamble in Qatar's history. The state's finances were strained, and the global market for gas remained uncertain. The technology required to produce and export Liquefied Natural Gas (LNG)—gas chilled to -162°C until it becomes a liquid, reducing its volume 600-fold for transport by sea—was in its infancy. Building the offshore platforms, pipelines, and onshore liquefaction plants would require an upfront investment of many billions of dollars. Many international energy experts and financial institutions were deeply skeptical, viewing the project as a potential white elephant that could bankrupt the small nation.

Despite the immense risks, Sheikh Khalifa's government concluded that it had no other choice. To do nothing was to accept a future of dwindling oil revenues and inevitable economic decline. In 1984, the state established the Qatar Liquefied Gas Company Ltd., or Qatargas, a joint venture between the state-owned Qatar General Petroleum Corporation (QGPC), and foreign partners. Bringing in international oil companies like Total of France, Mobil of the U.S., and Japan's Marubeni and Mitsui was crucial. They possessed the technology, the project management expertise, and, most importantly, the access to global markets that Qatar lacked.

The development was planned in three phases. The first, and most straightforward, was the Alpha Project. Sanctioned in 1987, its primary goal was to produce gas for Qatar's own domestic needs. An offshore production complex was built some 80 kilometers from the coast, linked by pipeline to the industrial city of Mesaieed. Production began in 1991, and the gas was used to power the country's electricity grids, run its water desalination plants, and provide feedstock for its fertilizer and petrochemical industries. The Alpha Project was a crucial first step, a way to begin monetizing the field while proving the technology and building local expertise.

The second and third phases were far more ambitious and represented the heart of the gas revolution: producing LNG for export. This was where the real gamble lay. An LNG project is an integrated chain of staggering complexity, from the wellhead to the end user. It requires not only the liquefaction plant but also a fleet of highly specialized, cryogenic tanker ships and dedicated receiving terminals in the destination country. The entire chain costs billions of dollars and is only financially viable if a buyer is willing to sign a long-term contract, typically for 20 to 25 years, guaranteeing to purchase the LNG. Without a signed Sales and Purchase Agreement (SPA), no bank would finance such a colossal undertaking. The search for a buyer was on.

The focus of this search was singular: Japan. As an industrial powerhouse with almost no domestic energy resources, Japan had been an early adopter of LNG in the 1970s, seeking to diversify its energy mix away from oil and coal for both security and environmental reasons. It was the world's largest and most established LNG market, and securing a Japanese customer was the key to unlocking the entire North Field project. The negotiations were painstaking and protracted. The Japanese utility companies were famously tough negotiators, demanding reliability and competitive pricing. For Qatar, a newcomer to the LNG game with no track record, it was a hard sell.

The breakthrough came in 1992. After years of talks, Qatargas signed a landmark SPA with the Chubu Electric Power Company, one of Japan's largest utilities. The agreement committed Chubu to purchase four million tonnes of LNG per year for a period of 25 years, starting in 1997. This was the moment the gas revolution became real. The Chubu contract was the foundation stone, the bankable guarantee that allowed Qatargas to secure the necessary financing for the project. In 1994, a second agreement was signed with a consortium of seven other Japanese gas and utility companies, bringing the total commitment to six million tonnes per year.

With the contracts in hand, Qatar and its partners could finally approach the financial markets. The Japanese government played a critical role, with the Japanese Export-Import Bank providing the bulk of the financing for the initial liquefaction plant, a sum of $1.6 billion. Japanese firms were deeply involved in every stage, from investing in the project to building the plant and the specialized ships needed to transport the gas. The financing for the first two "trains"—the massive industrial units that liquefy the gas—was finalized in December 1993.

While Qatargas was securing its first customers, the government was already planning the next stage of expansion. In 1993, a second LNG venture, Ras Laffan Liquefied Natural Gas Company (RasGas), was established as a joint venture between QGPC and the American oil giant Mobil. Mobil's involvement brought significant financial muscle and technical expertise, and crucially, provided the political security of having a major U.S. company deeply invested in Qatar's future. In 1995, RasGas secured its own foundational customer, signing a 25-year SPA to supply 2.4 million tonnes of LNG per year to the Korea Gas Corporation (KOGAS).

To house this new industry, Qatar embarked on one of the most ambitious construction projects in its history. The decision was made to build an entirely new industrial city from scratch on a desolate stretch of coastline at the northeastern tip of the peninsula, chosen for its proximity to the offshore field. This site was named Ras Laffan. Starting in 1991, work began to dredge a massive artificial harbor, which would become the largest in the world, and to build the infrastructure for the sprawling liquefaction plants. In 1993, the contract to construct the first Qatargas LNG plant was awarded to Japan's Chiyoda Corporation, and the first heavy equipment began arriving at the new port a year later.

As the decade progressed, the empty coastline at Ras Laffan was transformed into a city of steel, a forest of cooling towers, storage tanks, and processing units. The scale of the engineering was monumental. It was a declaration of intent, a physical manifestation of Qatar's bet on a gas-powered future. The first shipment of condensate, a valuable liquid hydrocarbon stripped from the gas, left the new port in 1996. The climax of this first, daring phase of the revolution arrived in late December of that year, when the brand-new, purpose-built LNG tanker, *Al Zubarah*, docked at the newly completed terminal. On December 23, 1996, it sailed for Japan with Qatar's first-ever cargo of liquefied natural gas, destined for Chubu Electric.

That first shipment was the culmination of a decade of high-stakes diplomacy, complex engineering, and audacious financial risk-taking. Sheikh Khalifa's government had taken the country to the brink, betting its entire sovereign wealth on a project many believed was doomed to fail. As the *Al Zubarah* steamed toward the Pacific, it carried more than just a cargo of super-chilled gas; it carried the future of Qatar.

CHAPTER SEVENTEEN: The 1995 Palace Coup and the Rise of Sheikh Hamad bin Khalifa Al Thani

By the early 1990s, Qatar was a nation holding its breath. The entire country was staked on a single, monumental gamble: the development of the North Field. The project was a leviathan, a multi-billion-dollar undertaking that was stretching the state's finances to their absolute limit. Every available riyal was being poured into the construction of a vast industrial city at Ras Laffan, a fleet of specialized ships, and the colossal liquefaction plants needed to bring the gas to market. The man who had sanctioned this audacious bet, the Emir Sheikh Khalifa bin Hamad Al Thani, was a ruler of the old school. He had guided Qatar through independence and the first oil boom with a steady, cautious hand, preferring a quiet foreign policy and a traditional, patriarchal style of governance. Now in his sixties, he was increasingly detached from the daily grind of this complex new enterprise, often spending long stretches of the year in Europe.

The day-to-day responsibility for this high-stakes venture, and indeed for most of the country's affairs, had long since fallen to his son and Heir Apparent, Sheikh Hamad bin Khalifa Al Thani. Born in 1952, Sheikh Hamad was a product of a different era. Educated at the British Royal Military Academy at Sandhurst, he had served as Qatar's Minister of Defense since 1977, building the country's modern armed forces into a capable and loyal institution. He was energetic, hands-on, and deeply involved in the intricate negotiations with international energy companies, banks, and Japanese customers that were the lifeblood of the LNG project. While his father saw the gas as a necessary replacement for dwindling oil revenues, Sheikh Hamad saw it as something more: a strategic tool that could launch Qatar onto the world stage.

This divergence in vision between the aging, conservative father and the ambitious, dynamic son created a quiet but profound tension at the heart of the Qatari state. It was an open secret in Doha and in the boardrooms of international oil companies that while Sheikh Khalifa reigned, Sheikh Hamad ruled. He was the one who pushed for the creation of the second gas venture, RasGas, with the American company Mobil, a move that deepened ties with the United States. He was the one who grasped the sheer scale of the wealth that was about to flow and understood that it required a new, more modern, and more transparent style of governance. The old system, where state revenues were often indistinguishable from the ruler's private purse, was ill-suited to managing a multi-billion-dollar global industry.

The situation was becoming increasingly dysfunctional. The Emir was frequently absent, while the Heir Apparent was making the critical decisions that would define the nation's future. The country had, in effect, two centers of power, one de jure and often in Geneva, the other de facto and in Doha. For the international partners and financiers who had staked billions on Qatar's stability, this ambiguity was a source of concern. As the first LNG production loomed, the need for clear, decisive, and consistent leadership was paramount. Sheikh Hamad and his supporters within the ruling family concluded that the nation could no longer afford this dual authority. A change was necessary, not just for the success of the gas project, but for the future of the country.

The moment came on June 27, 1995. Sheikh Khalifa was in Zurich, Switzerland, having recently arrived for his annual summer stay. Back in Doha, the final preparations were made with quiet efficiency. The move was carefully orchestrated to be a seamless and bloodless transition, a family matter to be settled internally. Key members of the armed forces and security services, institutions that Sheikh Hamad had commanded for nearly two decades, secured strategic locations. The country's air and sea ports were temporarily closed, and telecommunication links were cut.

In the morning, Sheikh Hamad convened a meeting of the most senior members of the Al Thani family, alongside prominent tribal leaders and notable citizens. In the traditional manner, he informed them of the decision and received their pledges of allegiance, the *bay'ah*, recognizing him as the new Emir. The entire process was over within a few hours. There was no resistance and no public disorder. By midday, the state-run Qatar Television and Radio broadcast the official announcement. The announcer read a statement from the ruling family declaring that they had decided to "relieve His Highness Sheikh Khalifa bin Hamad Al Thani of his post" and had "pledged allegiance to Sheikh Hamad bin Khalifa Al Thani as Emir of the country."

The broadcast was followed by an address from the new Emir himself. Sheikh Hamad appeared on television, dressed in traditional robes, and spoke to the nation in calm, measured tones. "I am not happy with what has happened," he stated, acknowledging the gravity of deposing his own father, "but it had to be done and I had to do it." He outlined his vision for a new chapter in Qatar's history, promising reform, development, and a more prominent role for the country in the world. He reassured the public and the international community of his commitment to stability and continuity.

The reaction from the deposed Emir was swift and defiant. From his suite at the Baur au Lac hotel in Zurich, Sheikh Khalifa spoke to the international media, condemning the takeover. "What happened is very strange and unexpected," he told the BBC. "It's an abnormal behavior… what my son has done is against Islamic and civil law." He vowed that he was "going back to Qatar, whatever the cost." This vow, however, was quickly rendered moot by the realities of geopolitics. The transition in Doha was a fait accompli, and the international community, prioritizing stability in the Gulf, moved quickly to recognize the new reality.

Crucially, the first and most important blessing came from Saudi Arabia. King Fahd sent a congratulatory cable, a powerful signal to the rest of the region. The other GCC states swiftly followed suit. Recognition from the United States, Great Britain, and France was not far behind. They knew Sheikh Hamad well; he was the man they had been dealing with for years. His accession was seen not as a destabilizing coup, but as the formalization of an existing power structure, one that would ensure the security of their massive energy investments.

With his political position secure, Sheikh Hamad's first and most urgent challenge was financial. The deposed Emir had not only been the head of state but had also controlled vast state funds held in what were effectively personal accounts around the world. Estimates of the sums involved ran into the billions of dollars. With Sheikh Khalifa now in exile and refusing to relinquish control of these assets, the Qatari state, already highly leveraged to pay for the gas projects, faced a potential liquidity crisis. The new government was forced to launch a series of complex and protracted international legal proceedings to freeze and recover the funds. This financial struggle became a dominant theme of Sheikh Hamad's first year in power, a high-stakes battle fought in the courts of London, Paris, and Switzerland for the very capital needed to build Qatar's future. The state was forced to take on additional loans and even issue bonds to bridge the gap, a clear sign of the financial strain.

While the lawyers fought in Europe, Sheikh Khalifa had not abandoned his hope of a return. From exile, first in France and later in the neighboring United Arab Emirates, he rallied a small group of loyalists, including some disaffected members of the ruling family and former officials. They began to plot a counter-coup, an armed attempt to reverse the events of June 1995 and restore the old Emir to power.

The attempt came on the night of February 14, 1996. The plan, according to the official Qatari investigation that followed, was for a column of armed Bedouin mercenaries to cross the border from Saudi Arabia and link up with conspirators within Qatar's security forces and tribal leadership. They were to attack key government installations and assassinate the new Emir and other senior figures, including the foreign minister. The plot was ambitious, but it was also deeply compromised. Qatar's intelligence services, likely with foreign assistance, had infiltrated the conspiracy.

On the night of the planned attack, the authorities moved decisively. Security forces loyal to Sheikh Hamad intercepted the plotters, and after a series of brief but intense firefights, the attempt was crushed. The border was sealed, and over the following days and weeks, hundreds of people were arrested, from foreign mercenaries to Qatari military officers and prominent tribal figures. The former minister of economy and finance, a close associate of the deposed Emir, was named as one of the ringleaders.

The failed counter-coup of 1996 was a pivotal moment. While the initial takeover had been bloodless, the attempt to reverse it was not. The foiling of the plot demonstrated Sheikh Hamad's firm grip on the state's security apparatus and his government's resolve. The subsequent trial of the conspirators, which resulted in numerous prison sentences, effectively broke the back of the opposition and consolidated the new Emir's power. The episode also cast a chill over Qatar's relations with some of its neighbors, who were suspected of having turned a blind eye, or even offered support, to the plotters. It was a stark lesson for the new leadership that Qatar's newfound assertiveness could generate friction within the ostensibly unified brotherhood of the GCC.

With his rule now uncontested, Sheikh Hamad was free to accelerate the profound transformation of Qatar he had long envisioned. The change in leadership was not merely cosmetic; it was a fundamental shift in philosophy. The cautious, insular Qatar of Sheikh Khalifa was to be replaced by a new Qatar: dynamic, outward-looking, and determined to use its immense gas wealth to punch far above its demographic weight. The first shipment of LNG to Japan, which sailed from Ras Laffan in December 1996, was more than a commercial milestone; it was the financial fuel for this new ambition. Sheikh Hamad, now firmly in control, had secured the country's economic future. He would now begin the work of building its political and cultural influence, a project that would soon make the small peninsula a household name across the globe.

CHAPTER EIGHTEEN: Al Jazeera and the New Public Diplomacy: Qatar on the World Stage

The Qatar that Sheikh Hamad bin Khalifa Al Thani now commanded in the summer of 1995 was on the cusp of unimaginable wealth, but in the court of global opinion, it was a near-total unknown. To the extent that it registered at all, it was seen as a sleepy, conservative Gulf sheikhdom, a dusty peninsula whose primary function was to serve as a reliable, if minor, supplier of crude oil. The new Emir, however, had a vision that went far beyond the role of a quiet gas station attendant. He understood that in the modern world, true security for a small state came not just from military alliances, but from relevance. To survive and prosper in a neighborhood of giants, Qatar needed to be noticed. It needed a voice. It needed influence. The first shipments of liquefied natural gas would provide the money to pursue this ambition; a fortuitous corporate collapse in London would provide the means.

In April 1996, a high-profile joint venture between the British Broadcasting Corporation (BBC) and a Saudi-owned company, Orbit Communications, to create a BBC Arabic television news service, dramatically imploded. The partnership had been fraught from the start, a clash between the BBC's fiercely guarded editorial independence and the Saudi government's intolerance for any critical coverage of its affairs, particularly its human rights record. When the BBC aired a documentary critical of the Saudi justice system, the Saudi partners tried to censor it, and the entire enterprise fell apart. This left a highly skilled, Western-trained team of some 250 Arab journalists, producers, and technicians suddenly unemployed. For Sheikh Hamad, this was a golden opportunity.

He moved swiftly. An Emiri decree was issued, and with a start-up loan from the Emir himself of 500 million Qatari riyals (about

$137 million), a new satellite channel was born. Much of the staff from the defunct BBC service was hired en masse, bringing with them a professional ethos of investigative journalism and critical inquiry that was utterly alien to the media landscape of the Middle East. On November 1, 1996, the Al Jazeera Satellite Channel—the name meaning "The Peninsula" in Arabic—went on the air for the first time, broadcasting six hours a day from a modest set of studios in Doha.

What followed was nothing short of a cultural and political earthquake. For decades, the Arab world had been fed a relentlessly monotonous media diet of fawning coverage of the local ruler, heavily censored news, and bland cultural programming. Al Jazeera shattered this mold. It was loud, argumentative, and deliberately provocative. Its now-famous motto was "The Opinion and the Other Opinion" (Al-Ra'y wa-al-Ra'y al-Akhar), and it took this philosophy to heart. The channel gave airtime to long-silenced opposition figures, government critics, and controversial intellectuals from across the political spectrum. In a move that was utterly shocking to many Arab viewers, it regularly featured Israeli officials and commentators, forcing audiences to hear directly from a voice they had only ever known through the filter of hostile state propaganda.

The network's signature programs became required viewing and a source of constant uproar. The most famous was a weekly debate show hosted by the acerbic Syrian-born academic Faisal al-Qassem, called "The Opposite Direction" (Al-Ittijah al-Mu'akis). The show's format was brutally simple: pit two guests with diametrically opposed views on a hot-button political or social issue against each other and let them argue, often at the top of their lungs, for an hour. It was political theater of the highest order, tackling taboo subjects like democracy, corruption, and the role of religion in society. Viewers were transfixed. For the first time, they were seeing the kind of raucous, open debate that was commonplace in Western parliaments but unheard of in the tightly controlled public sphere of the Arab world.

The "Al Jazeera effect," as it came to be known, was immediate. The channel's popularity soared, particularly among ordinary citizens who were starved for information and tired of the condescending propaganda of their own state media. For the rulers of the region, however, it was a nightmare. Accustomed to a media that served as a loyal arm of the state, they were suddenly faced with a Qatar-funded channel that was airing their dirty laundry, interviewing their most vocal critics, and stirring up public debate they could not control.

The diplomatic backlash was swift and furious. One by one, Arab governments began to register their official displeasure. Ambassadors were recalled for "consultations," a common diplomatic signal of extreme irritation. Al Jazeera's bureaus were periodically shut down in capitals across the region, its journalists harassed or denied credentials. The complaints directed at Sheikh Hamad's government were relentless. In 2002, the simmering anger boiled over when Saudi Arabia, infuriated by the channel's coverage of the Kingdom, withdrew its ambassador from Doha for what would become a six-year period. Similar diplomatic protests came from Egypt, Jordan, Kuwait, and Bahrain. Sheikh Hamad and his foreign minister, the equally assertive Sheikh Hamad bin Jassim Al Thani, weathered the storm, consistently repeating the mantra that the channel was editorially independent. This claim was met with widespread skepticism, given that the station relied on government funding, yet the sheer novelty and audacity of the project gave it a unique power.

Al Jazeera was the most spectacular, but by no means the only, element of a sophisticated new Qatari foreign policy. Sheikh Hamad's strategy was to transform Qatar from a passive Saudi satellite state into an active, independent player. Recognizing Qatar's inherent vulnerabilities—its small size and indefensible geography—he pursued a multi-pronged strategy to make his country indispensable. This strategy had two core components that often seemed to be in direct contradiction with each other.

The first component was a deep and binding security relationship with the United States. While Sheikh Jassim had invited the

Ottomans in to balance the British a century earlier, Sheikh Hamad invited the Americans in to balance his powerful regional neighbors. In 1996, the same year Al Jazeera was launched, Qatar built the massive Al Udeid Air Base at a cost of over $1 billion. When the U.S. needed to relocate its regional Combat Air Operations Center out of Saudi Arabia after the 9/11 attacks due to political sensitivities, Qatar eagerly offered up the state-of-the-art facility. Al Udeid soon became the forward headquarters of U.S. Central Command, the nerve center for American air operations across a vast swath of the globe, including the wars in Afghanistan and Iraq.

The second component of the strategy was a policy of "open doors" and active mediation. While hosting America's most important airbase in the region, Qatar also deliberately cultivated relationships with a dizzying array of actors, many of whom were on Washington's blacklists. Doha became a place where everyone, regardless of their ideology, could talk. It maintained cordial relations with Iran, its giant neighbor across the Gulf. It engaged with Islamist groups like the Muslim Brotherhood and hosted exiled leaders from Hamas.

This unique position, of being a trusted U.S. military ally that also kept lines of communication open to America's adversaries, allowed Qatar to carve out a niche as the region's indispensable mediator. Sheikh Hamad's government began to actively involve itself in conflict resolution, leveraging its immense wealth and its carefully cultivated neutrality to broker deals. In the late 1990s and early 2000s, Qatar began mediating in disputes from Sudan to Lebanon, a role that would grow dramatically in the coming years.

This dual-track foreign policy created a series of paradoxes that often bewildered outside observers. The same country hosting the U.S. Air Force was also home to a television network that many in the U.S. government viewed as virulently anti-American. The relationship became particularly strained after the September 11, 2001 attacks. Al Jazeera was the only international network with a functioning bureau in Taliban-controlled Afghanistan, and as a result, it became the exclusive conduit for video messages from Osama bin Laden and other al-Qaeda leaders.

To American officials prosecuting the "War on Terror," this was tantamount to giving a platform to terrorists. Secretary of Defense Donald Rumsfeld and Secretary of State Colin Powell publicly castigated the network, with Rumsfeld branding its coverage "propagandistic and inflammatory." U.S. officials repeatedly and unsuccessfully pressured the Qatari government to rein in the channel. The situation was surreal: in Washington, senior officials were condemning Al Jazeera's broadcasts, while in the Qatari desert, American generals at Al Udeid were planning bombing runs.

For Qatar, this was not a contradiction; it was the very essence of its survival strategy. The American security umbrella provided the "hard power" protection it needed, while Al Jazeera and its hyperactive diplomacy provided the "soft power" that made it a player. By making itself the home of both the U.S. military's command center and the Arab world's most influential media outlet, Qatar had made itself too important, and too useful, to be ignored or bullied by its larger neighbors.

Within a few short years of Sheikh Hamad's accession, Qatar had been utterly rebranded. It was no longer a quiet backwater. It was now the home of Al Jazeera, a revolutionary media force that was reshaping the political discourse of an entire region. It was a key American ally, a hub for international diplomacy, and a nation that was deliberately, and often controversially, punching far above its weight. This new, assertive posture was not without its risks. It generated enormous friction with its neighbors and complicated its relationship with its primary protector. But it had achieved the new Emir's primary objective: in the crowded and dangerous theater of Middle Eastern politics, Qatar had decisively stepped out of the shadows and onto the world stage.

CHAPTER NINETEEN: Economic Diversification and the Qatar National Vision 2030

The first LNG tanker that sailed from Ras Laffan in December 1996 was a vessel of destiny. It carried not just a cargo of super-chilled gas, but the financial fuel for a national reinvention of breathtaking ambition. The Qatar of the late 1990s, with Sheikh Hamad bin Khalifa Al Thani now firmly at the helm, was a country grappling with a paradox of prosperity. The North Field had secured the nation's wealth for generations, a geological lottery win of epic proportions. Yet, this very success highlighted a profound vulnerability. The entire edifice of the modern Qatari state—its welfare system, its security, its burgeoning international profile—rested on the single, volatile pillar of the global energy market. The leadership understood, with the clarity that only a history of pearling collapse can provide, that to rely on a single commodity, no matter how valuable, was to build a palace on a foundation of sand.

The idea of diversification was not new. The industrial cities of Mesaieed and Ras Laffan, with their steel mills, fertilizer plants, and petrochemical complexes, were the first-generation attempts to move beyond the simple extraction and sale of raw hydrocarbons. They were a crucial first step, transforming gas molecules into higher-value products. But Sheikh Hamad's vision was grander and more radical. He sought not just to industrialize the economy, but to fundamentally rewire it. The goal was to transform Qatar from a state that *sells* a resource into a nation that *provides* services, *creates* knowledge, and *acts* as a global hub for commerce, finance, and transportation. The immense LNG revenues were not an end in themselves; they were the seed capital for a post-hydrocarbon future.

One of the earliest and most visible pillars of this new strategy was the creation of a world-class national airline. The original Qatar

Airways, a small regional carrier, was relaunched in 1997 with a new mandate and a virtually unlimited budget. The strategy, spearheaded by a new management team, was audacious: to build a global airline that could compete with the established giants of the industry. The government embarked on a massive fleet expansion, placing multi-billion-dollar orders for the latest aircraft from Airbus and Boeing. The airline's strategy was to leverage Qatar's geographic position, turning Doha into a major intercontinental transit hub, a "super-connector" linking Europe, Asia, Africa, and the Americas. Qatar Airways was conceived as more than a business; it was a tool of soft power, a flying ambassador for a nation determined to put itself on the map. Every aircraft with the familiar oryx on its tail flying into Heathrow, JFK, or Narita was a projection of the new Qatar's global ambition.

While the airline conquered the skies, another initiative sought to capture the global flow of capital. In 2005, the government established the Qatar Financial Centre (QFC). This was not merely a new business district; it was an entirely separate legal and regulatory jurisdiction carved out within the state. The QFC operated under a legal framework based on English common law, with its own courts and regulatory bodies, all designed to be familiar and reassuring to international banks, insurance companies, and asset management firms. It was a direct and ambitious attempt to compete with established regional financial hubs like Bahrain and the rapidly growing Dubai International Financial Centre. The QFC was a signal to the world that Qatar was not just a place to extract resources, but a safe and sophisticated place to do business.

This new economy needed a new physical environment. The dusty, low-rise Doha of the 1980s was ill-suited to the image of a gleaming global hub. The government and its related entities embarked on a series of mega-projects designed to transform the urban landscape. The most spectacular of these was The Pearl-Qatar, a vast man-made island built on reclaimed land off the coast of Doha. Designed to resemble a string of pearls, it was a multi-billion-dollar development of high-rise towers, luxury villas, marinas, and high-end retail, all built in a pastiche of Mediterranean styles. Crucially, it was the first piece of land in Qatar where freehold ownership was available to foreign nationals. The Pearl was more than a real estate project; it was a magnet for foreign capital and a lifestyle destination designed to attract the highly paid expatriate professionals needed to run the new, knowledge-based industries. It was followed by the even more ambitious plan for Lusail City, a completely new, planned metropolis north of Doha, envisioned as a "smart city" of the future.

By the mid-2000s, these disparate, high-octane initiatives were rapidly changing the face of the country. A new skyline was rising, a new airline was circling the globe, and new financial regulations were being written. Yet, it was becoming apparent that this frantic activity needed a coherent, overarching framework. The country needed a roadmap, a shared national purpose that could guide its development, channel its immense wealth, and manage the profound social transformations that were underway.

This realization led to the most comprehensive planning exercise in the nation's history. Under the guidance of the General Secretariat for Development Planning, the state embarked on a years-long process of consultation with government agencies, the private sector, and civil society to create a long-term blueprint for the nation's future. The result, unveiled by Emiri decree in October 2008, was the Qatar National Vision 2030 (QNV 2030).

The Vision was far more than a simple economic plan. It was a holistic social contract, a foundational document that sought to answer the fundamental question: what kind of country did Qatar want to be by the year 2030? Its stated goal was to transform Qatar into "an advanced society capable of sustaining its development and providing a high standard of living for all of its people." The document was candid about the challenges, acknowledging the country's overreliance on hydrocarbons, the environmental stress of rapid development, and the profound social challenges posed by a majority-expatriate population. To address these, the Vision was built upon four interconnected pillars, each representing a core component of the nation's future.

The first pillar was Human Development, a recognition that the country's most valuable resource was not the gas under the ground, but the people living on it. The goal was to build a well-educated and healthy population, capable of participating in a competitive global economy. This pillar called for a complete overhaul of the education system to foster creative and analytical thinking, and the creation of a world-class healthcare system that was both preventative and curative. It was a declaration that the state's role was not just to distribute wealth, but to empower its citizens to create their own.

The second pillar, Social Development, tackled the complex challenge of building a modern, just, and safe society while preserving its deep-rooted cultural and religious traditions. It was an attempt to navigate the treacherous currents of globalization without losing the nation's soul. This pillar emphasized the importance of the family as the core social unit, promoted tolerance and openness to other cultures, and articulated a goal of increasing the participation of Qatari women in all spheres of life. It also called for the promotion of a vibrant cultural scene and the development of world-class sports facilities, seeing these as vital for fostering a sense of national identity and pride.

The third, and arguably most central, pillar was Economic Development. This was the engine of the entire Vision, the plan to build a diversified and sustainable economy. Its core objective was the responsible management of the nation's hydrocarbon wealth, using the revenues to build a future where the economy was driven by knowledge and private enterprise. The strategy outlined a shift away from a state-dominated economy to one where a thriving private sector, both local and foreign, would be the main driver of growth. It called for the creation of a business-friendly environment that would attract foreign investment and technology, and identified key sectors for development, including finance, tourism, and services. The ultimate goal was to ensure economic prosperity long after the last gas tanker had sailed.

The final pillar was Environmental Development, a frank acknowledgement that Qatar's rapid rise had come at a significant environmental cost. The nation had one of the highest per capita carbon footprints in the world, its groundwater was being depleted, and its marine and coastal ecosystems were under severe stress from land reclamation and industrial activity. This pillar committed the state to balancing the needs of development with the protection of the environment. It called for the formulation of urban development plans that would be less taxing on natural resources, the promotion of environmental awareness, and investment in green technologies. It was a recognition that long-term sustainability could not be purely economic; it had to be environmental as well.

To ensure that the lofty goals of the Vision were translated into concrete action, the government introduced a system of medium-term National Development Strategies (NDS). The first of these, covering the period from 2011 to 2016, was launched in March 2011. The NDS was the practical implementation plan, the "how-to" guide that broke down the Vision's grand aspirations into specific programs, projects, and policy initiatives, complete with budgets and measurable targets. It was the NDS that would authorize the funding for the new hospitals, the curriculum reforms, the infrastructure projects like the Doha Metro, and the environmental regulations that would make the Vision a reality.

Underpinning this entire diversification strategy was another powerful new entity, the financial engine designed to secure Qatar's future in the global marketplace. In 2005, the government established the Qatar Investment Authority (QIA), a sovereign wealth fund tasked with investing the state's massive hydrocarbon surplus. The QIA's mission was twofold: first, to generate a steady stream of income that would one day replace the revenue from oil and gas, and second, to make strategic investments that could support Qatar's own domestic development by bringing in new technologies and expertise.

Operating with a level of financial firepower that made it one of the most formidable players in global finance, the QIA quickly began to acquire a portfolio of trophy assets and strategic stakes in blue-chip companies. It bought the iconic London department store Harrods, financed The Shard, Western Europe's tallest skyscraper, and acquired significant holdings in global brands like Volkswagen, Barclays Bank, and the London Stock Exchange. In a move that signaled the growing link between finance and soft power, a subsidiary of the QIA purchased the French football club Paris Saint-Germain in 2011, transforming it overnight into one of the wealthiest clubs in the world. These high-profile acquisitions were more than just investments; they were a form of national branding, a way of embedding the name of Qatar into the fabric of the global economy and culture. The QIA was diversifying the nation's wealth by buying a piece of the world itself, ensuring that even when the gas boom subsided, Qatar would remain a global player.

CHAPTER TWENTY: Education City and the Knowledge Economy

The vast revenues unlocked by the North Field presented Qatar's leadership with a question as profound as it was practical: what does a country do when it has more money than it knows what to do with? For the Emir, Sheikh Hamad bin Khalifa Al Thani, and his wife, Sheikha Moza bint Nasser, the answer was clear. The gas wealth was a finite blessing, a temporary gift of geology that had to be converted into something permanent and self-sustaining. The ultimate goal, as enshrined in the National Vision 2030, was to transition from an economy based on carbon to one based on the human mind. The central pillar of this audacious strategy was an idea so bold it bordered on the fantastical: to build, from scratch, a global hub of elite learning in the middle of the desert.

This was not to be a single, national university, but something entirely new. The plan was to import education wholesale, to persuade some of the world's most prestigious universities to establish full-fledged branch campuses in Qatar. The model was simple, if astronomically expensive: Qatar would pay for everything—the land, the state-of-the-art buildings, the faculty salaries, the operational costs, even the student scholarships. In return, the universities would bring their curricula, their academic standards, their brand names, and their degrees. It was a strategy of buying, not building, an entire world-class higher education sector.

The vehicle for this grand experiment was the Qatar Foundation for Education, Science and Community Development (QF), a private, non-profit organization established by Emiri decree in 1995. While the Emir provided the vision and the financial backing, the driving force and public face of the Foundation was Sheikha Moza. Her personal passion and tireless advocacy transformed the Qatar Foundation from a concept into a sprawling, multi-billion-dollar reality. QF's mandate extended far beyond just universities, but its flagship project, the one that would define its global identity, was a 12-square-kilometer patch of desert on the outskirts of Doha that was given a simple, aspirational name: Education City.

The first step was to prove the concept was viable. In 1998, after being launched by the Qatar Foundation a year prior, Virginia Commonwealth University, an American institution renowned for its arts and design programs, agreed to open a branch campus. VCU School of the Arts in Qatar became the pioneer, the first international university to plant its flag in Education City. Its initial focus on arts and design was a strategic choice, seen as a culturally appropriate and less controversial field to begin with, particularly for encouraging the enrollment of Qatari women.

If VCU was the proof of concept, the next step was the game-changer. In 2001, after extensive negotiations, the Qatar Foundation signed a landmark agreement with one of the most prestigious universities in the United States: Cornell University. The deal to establish the Weill Cornell Medical College in Qatar was a coup of the highest order. It was the first time an American medical school had ever opened a branch campus overseas, and the fact that an Ivy League institution was willing to award its M.D. degree in Doha gave the entire Education City project immense and immediate credibility. With an estimated operating budget of $750 million for its first decade, fully funded by QF, the scale of Qatar's ambition was made clear. The first pre-medical students were admitted in 2002, marking the first co-educational higher learning institute in the country's history.

The Cornell deal opened the floodgates. Over the next few years, a carefully curated portfolio of elite American universities was assembled, each chosen to fill a specific niche in the new knowledge economy. In 2003, Texas A&M University arrived, bringing its top-ranked engineering programs, vital for a nation whose economy was still fundamentally based on hydrocarbon extraction and processing. Carnegie Mellon University followed in 2004, offering programs in business administration and computer science, the building blocks of a modern, digitized economy. In 2005, Georgetown University's School of Foreign Service opened its doors, a clear signal of Qatar's ambition to train its own generation of diplomats and foreign policy experts to navigate its increasingly complex role on the world stage. Northwestern University, with its famed journalism school, joined in 2008, a logical fit for a country that was already home to Al Jazeera and sought to become a global media hub.

As the roster of universities grew, so did the physical campus itself. Education City was transformed into an architectural showcase, a statement written in glass, steel, and intricately carved stone. World-renowned architects were commissioned to design buildings that were both functional and iconic. The result was a stunning, otherworldly landscape of futuristic structures rising from the desert floor, a stark contrast to the traditional architecture of old Doha. This was a purpose-built environment, designed to foster collaboration and inspire innovation, a physical manifestation of the country's forward-looking aspirations. Officially inaugurated in 2003, the city had evolved from a single school into a diverse campus hosting students from over 50 nations.

The vision for Education City, however, was always more than just a collection of foreign teaching outposts. The ultimate goal was to create a complete, self-sustaining ecosystem of knowledge, from primary school to post-doctoral research. Even before the first university arrived, QF had established Qatar Academy in 1995, a private K-12 school designed to provide a high-quality, bilingual education that could prepare local students for the rigors of the elite universities to come. An Academic Bridge Program was added in 2001, offering a foundation year for high school graduates who needed to bolster their English and academic skills to meet the demanding entrance requirements of the partner universities.

Crucially, the leadership understood that a true knowledge economy could not be based on teaching alone; it required a robust culture of research and development. To that end, the Qatar Foundation created two vital, complementary institutions. The first was the Qatar National Research Fund (QNRF), established in 2006. The QNRF was tasked with a simple but essential mission:

to build a culture of research from the ground up by providing competitive funding for projects across all disciplines, from medicine and engineering to the humanities and arts. It was designed to act as a catalyst, encouraging original, locally relevant research and fostering partnerships between academia and industry.

The second institution was the physical hub designed to make those partnerships happen: the Qatar Science & Technology Park (QSTP). Inaugurated in 2009 with an initial investment of over $800 million, QSTP was established as a free-trade zone adjacent to the university campuses. Its purpose was to be the bridge between academia and the commercial world. QSTP provided state-of-the-art labs and office space to attract the research and development arms of major international technology companies, such as Microsoft, Shell, and General Electric, encouraging them to set up shop in Qatar and collaborate with the faculty and students next door. It also served as a technology incubator, providing funding and mentorship to help local start-ups transform promising ideas into commercially viable products.

The capstone of this integrated system of health, education, and research was to be the Sidra Medical and Research Center. First announced in 2004, Sidra was envisioned as an ultra-modern, all-digital academic hospital specializing in the care of women and children. Funded by a then-unprecedented endowment of $7.9 billion from the Qatar Foundation, it was designed to be the primary clinical and teaching partner for Weill Cornell Medical College, a place where the next generation of doctors would be trained and where cutting-edge biomedical research would be conducted. The project's development was long and complex, but its ambition was clear: to position Qatar as a regional leader in specialized healthcare and to help build the country's scientific expertise.

This entire, breathtakingly ambitious project was not without its challenges and critics. The cost was astronomical, with billions of dollars spent on a model whose long-term sustainability was unproven. Questions were raised about the appropriateness of

Western universities operating in a country with significant restrictions on freedom of speech and expression. Some wondered if transplanting the culture of American liberal arts education into the conservative social fabric of the Gulf was truly possible, or if the result would be a sanitized, self-censored version of the real thing. Inside Qatar, there were concerns that the system was creating a new, Westernized elite, disconnected from the mainstream of society that still attended the national, Arabic-language Qatar University.

There was also the practical challenge of finding enough qualified students. Despite being tuition-free for Qatari citizens, many of the programs initially struggled to attract local male students, with women making up the great majority of the student body. The universities relied heavily on expatriate and international students to fill their classrooms, raising questions about whether the primary goal of educating a new generation of Qataris was being fully met.

Despite these hurdles, the sheer scale and audacity of the project were undeniable. Within just over a decade, Qatar had built a globally recognized hub for higher education where none had existed before. It had deliberately chosen to invest its finite hydrocarbon wealth into what it saw as the only truly infinite resource: human capital. Education City was the physical embodiment of the Qatar National Vision 2030, a bet that the country's future would be secured not in the gas fields of the Persian Gulf, but in the lecture halls, libraries, and laboratories rising from the desert sand.

CHAPTER TWENTY-ONE: Hosting the World: The 2006 Asian Games and the Bid for the World Cup

By the turn of the millennium, Qatar's reinvention under Sheikh Hamad bin Khalifa Al Thani was proceeding at a blistering pace. Al Jazeera was reshaping the Arab public sphere, Education City was importing the infrastructure of a knowledge economy, and the Qatar Investment Authority was beginning to project the nation's financial power across the globe. Yet, for a country determined to become a global player, one crucial arena of soft power remained to be conquered: the world of major international sports. Sport, the Emir and his advisers understood, possessed a unique, unifying power. It transcended language, politics, and religion. To host a major sporting event was to invite the world to your home, to command its attention, and to shape its perceptions. It was the ultimate nation-branding exercise, and Qatar, with its boundless ambition and seemingly limitless budget, was ready to play.

The first great test of this new strategy was the 15th Asian Games, scheduled for December 2006. When Doha was selected as the host city by the Olympic Council of Asia in November 2000, beating out rivals like Kuala Lumpur and Hong Kong, many observers were skeptical. Qatar was the first Arab nation to be awarded the games, and only the second city in West Asia after Tehran in 1974. It was a country with a tiny native population and, at the time, a distinct lack of world-class sporting facilities. The pledge made during the bidding process was staggering: Qatar promised to spend whatever it took to build the necessary infrastructure from scratch.

What followed was a construction boom of epic proportions, a six-year national mobilization that dwarfed anything the country had undertaken before. The government committed a reported $2.8 billion to the games, a sum that would be used to transform the urban and sporting landscape of the country. The centerpiece of this effort was the Aspire Zone, a 2.5-square-kilometer "Sports City" that rose from the desert on the western edge of Doha. This vast complex included the Aspire Dome, the world's largest indoor multi-sport facility, and the Aspire Academy, a high-tech sports academy designed to identify and nurture future generations of Qatari athletes. The existing Khalifa International Stadium, the traditional home of Qatari football, underwent a massive renovation, its capacity more than doubled from 20,000 to 50,000 seats and a sweeping new arch and roof structure added to its profile. An entirely new Athletes' Village was constructed to house the more than 10,500 athletes and officials, and the Doha International Airport was significantly expanded to handle the influx of visitors.

As December 1, 2006, approached, the question was not whether Qatar could build the venues, but whether a country of its size could pull off an event of such complexity. The 15th Asian Games were the largest in history, featuring for the first time all 45 member nations of the Olympic Council of Asia, competing in 39 sports. It was, after the Summer Olympics, the second-biggest multi-sport event in the world.

The opening ceremony at the Khalifa International Stadium was Qatar's formal coming-out party. Produced by David Atkins, the man behind the Sydney 2000 Olympics ceremony, it was a breathtaking spectacle of light, sound, and pyrotechnics designed to showcase both Arab heritage and modern technological prowess. In front of a capacity crowd of 50,000, which included dignitaries like IOC President Jacques Rogge and Syrian President Bashar al-Assad, the ceremony unfolded as a grand narrative. A story of a "Seeker" traveling through Asia was told through massive video projections and elaborate performances featuring troupes of dancers, ornate caravans representing the regions of Asia, and a procession of 64 Arabian horsemen.

The climax of the ceremony, and its most unforgettable image, was the lighting of the games cauldron. The torch was carried into the stadium and passed to Sheikh Mohammed bin Hamad Al Thani, the Emir's son and captain of the Qatar equestrian team. In a stunning feat of horsemanship and engineering, he rode his horse up a steep, specially constructed ramp that seemed to rise to the very top of the stadium, lighting the giant cauldron against the night sky as fireworks erupted across the city. It was a moment of pure spectacle, a bold and unambiguous statement that Qatar had arrived on the world sporting stage.

The games themselves proceeded with remarkable efficiency. For fifteen days, Doha was the center of the Asian sporting world. Qatar had not only built the hardware; it had successfully managed the immense logistical software of transport, security, and accommodation. The event was a triumph of organization, proving to a global television audience estimated at 3 billion people that the small Gulf state was capable of executing a mega-event on a world-class scale. This success did not go unnoticed. FIFA President Sepp Blatter, watching from afar, would later cite Qatar's flawless hosting of the Asian Games as proof of its infrastructural and organizational capacity.

Having passed its first great test with flying colors, the Qatari leadership immediately set its sights on an even greater prize, the most watched, most prestigious, and most lucrative sporting event on Earth: the FIFA World Cup. The idea of a tiny desert nation with scorching summer heat and no discernible footballing history hosting the tournament seemed, to most of the world, utterly preposterous. But within the halls of power in Doha, it was the logical next step in the country's grand strategy.

In March 2009, Qatar officially submitted its bid to host the 2022 tournament. It was a crowded and formidable field of competitors. The United States, Australia, Japan, and South Korea were all in the race. Qatar was the unquestionable underdog, a David in a field of Goliaths. The bid was led by a team of young, Western-educated Qataris who embodied the new face of the nation. The Chairman was Sheikh Mohammed bin Hamad bin Khalifa Al Thani, the same young sheikh who had lit the Asian Games cauldron. The CEO was Hassan Al-Thawadi, a law graduate who was then serving as legal counsel for the Qatar Investment Authority.

Their strategy was to turn every perceived weakness into a strength. Too small? They pitched the first-ever "compact" World Cup, where all the stadiums would be within an hour's drive of each other, allowing fans to attend more than one match in a single day. No football heritage? They framed the bid as a historic opportunity to bring the World Cup to the Middle East for the first time, a chance to bridge cultural divides and create a legacy for a region of 450 million people.

The most significant and seemingly insurmountable obstacle was the climate. A World Cup is traditionally held in June and July, months when the temperature in Qatar routinely soars above 40°C (104°F), conditions considered dangerous for both players and fans. The bid committee's response to this challenge was its most audacious and technologically ambitious promise. They unveiled plans for a revolutionary, solar-powered cooling technology that would air-condition not only the stadiums but also fan zones and training sites, maintaining a comfortable temperature of around 20°C (68°F). This system, developed by engineers at Qatar University, would pump cool air through large nozzles at pitch level and smaller diffusers under each of the spectators' seats. It was a promise to air-condition the great outdoors, a solution so futuristic it bordered on science fiction.

The bid campaign, under the slogan "Expect Amazing," was a masterclass in modern public relations. Qatar leveraged its immense wealth to promote its message globally, hiring top international consulting firms and signing up global football icons like Zinedine Zidane and Pep Guardiola as ambassadors. The core message was consistent: this was a bid for the entire Arab world, a chance for FIFA to fulfill its motto, "For the Game, For the World," by taking a "bold gamble" and venturing into a new land.

As the campaign progressed, it was clear that Qatar was a serious contender, but few outside the bid team believed it could actually win. The technical inspection report from FIFA itself had flagged Qatar's bid as "high risk," citing the heat and the logistical challenges of building so much infrastructure from scratch. The United States, with its existing stadiums, massive commercial market, and successful hosting of the 1994 tournament, was widely considered the prohibitive favorite.

The final decision was to be made by the 22 members of the FIFA Executive Committee at the organization's headquarters in Zurich. On December 2, 2010, the delegations from the five bidding nations made their final, thirty-minute presentations. The Qatari presentation was a slick and emotionally resonant appeal, featuring a surprise appearance by Sheikha Moza bint Nasser, who spoke of what the World Cup would mean for the youth of the Middle East.

Later that afternoon, the 22 men of the executive committee cast their secret ballots. After four rounds of voting, the field was whittled down to a final two: the United States and Qatar. FIFA President Sepp Blatter took to the stage in the Zurich convention hall, a white envelope in his hand. He paused for dramatic effect, opened the envelope, and announced a result that sent a shockwave through the world of sport: "The winner to organize the 2022 FIFA World Cup is... Qatar."

The reaction in the hall was one of stunned disbelief. The Qatari delegation erupted in joyous, tearful celebration, while the American team, led by former President Bill Clinton, looked on in stony silence. Around the world, the news was greeted with a mixture of amazement and immediate, intense criticism. How could FIFA award its greatest prize to a tiny nation with no footballing tradition, where summer temperatures made playing the game impossible, and where a host of social and political questions remained unanswered?

For Qatar, however, it was the ultimate triumph. The audacious gamble had paid off. The years of planning, the billions spent on the Asian Games, and the relentless, globe-spanning diplomatic and marketing campaign had delivered the grandest prize of all. The country had successfully bid for and won the right to host the world. Now, it would have to build it.

CHAPTER TWENTY-TWO: The Arab Spring and Qatar's Foreign Policy

The final days of 2010 were a moment of supreme confidence for Qatar. The astonishing victory in the bid for the 2022 FIFA World Cup had capped a decade of hyper-ambitious projects that had propelled the tiny nation from obscurity to global recognition. Under the leadership of the Emir, Sheikh Hamad bin Khalifa Al Thani, and his equally formidable Prime Minister and Foreign Minister, Sheikh Hamad bin Jassim Al Thani, Qatar had cultivated a unique and often paradoxical foreign policy. It was simultaneously the host of America's largest regional airbase and the home of Al Jazeera, a media network that was a constant irritant to Washington and a mortal threat to the region's autocrats. This strategy of being indispensable to all sides had made Qatar a player, but it had also generated simmering resentment among its more traditional neighbors. The region was a brittle landscape of aging dictators, frustrated youth, and widespread corruption, a political order that seemed permanent, right up until the moment it was not.

The spark was lit not in a grand capital, but in the dusty Tunisian provincial town of Sidi Bouzid. On December 17, 2010, a 26-year-old street vendor named Mohamed Bouazizi, pushed to despair by the confiscation of his wares and the daily humiliations of a corrupt system, set himself on fire in front of the local governor's office. It was a tragic, solitary act of protest, the kind that might have gone unnoticed in another era. But in the age of mobile phones and satellite television, his sacrifice became a catalyst. Protests, fueled by years of pent-up anger over unemployment and oppression, erupted across Tunisia.

It was here that Al Jazeera came into its own. While state-run media across the Arab world ignored or downplayed the unrest, the Doha-based network provided saturation coverage. Its cameras broadcast the raw anger of the streets into living rooms from Rabat to Riyadh, turning a national uprising into a pan-Arab spectacle. It gave a platform to Tunisian activists, interviewed opposition figures, and framed the protests not as a riot, but as a legitimate struggle for dignity and freedom. For millions of viewers, it was a revelation. When Tunisia's long-serving president, Zine El Abidine Ben Ali, fled the country on January 14, 2011, after just four weeks of protests, the message was electrifying: the seemingly invincible regimes of the Arab world were, in fact, fragile. Qatar's government, reflecting the tone of its star media asset, quickly welcomed the change, signaling its support for the popular will.

If Tunisia was the spark, Egypt was the explosion. On January 25, 2011, inspired by the events in Tunisia, tens of thousands of Egyptians descended on Tahrir Square in central Cairo, demanding the downfall of Hosni Mubarak, who had ruled the most populous Arab nation for three decades. For eighteen days, the world was transfixed by the drama in the square, and Al Jazeera was its narrator. The network's live, 24-hour coverage became the revolution's soundtrack. Its journalists became participants in the story, their offices raided, their equipment confiscated, but their broadcasts continued, often through sheer ingenuity. The Egyptian state media portrayed the protesters as foreign agents and troublemakers; Al Jazeera portrayed them as heroes.

This divergence placed Qatar on a direct collision course with its most powerful neighbors. For Saudi Arabia and the United Arab Emirates, the fall of Mubarak was an unthinkable nightmare. He was a pillar of the regional order, a bulwark against Islamism, and a fellow autocrat. They threw their considerable diplomatic and financial weight behind him, viewing the uprising as a grave threat to their own stability. Qatar, in stark contrast, threw its weight behind the protesters. Its policy was a perfect alignment of its soft power tool, Al Jazeera, and its state interests. Supporting the revolution positioned Qatar as a progressive force on the side of the people, burnishing its global brand and distinguishing it from the sclerotic monarchies of the old guard. When Mubarak finally fell on February 11, Riyadh and Abu Dhabi were aghast. Doha was triumphant. Qatar moved quickly to embrace the new reality, pledging billions of dollars in aid and investment to the transitional government, and later to the democratically elected government led by the Muslim Brotherhood's Mohamed Morsi. It had placed a huge bet on a new, post-authoritarian Middle East, with political Islam as a dominant force.

The revolutionary contagion did not stop at Egypt's borders. In mid-February, protests erupted in the eastern Libyan city of Benghazi against the bizarre and brutal 42-year rule of Colonel Muammar Gaddafi. His response was swift and merciless. As his forces advanced on Benghazi, he delivered a rambling, terrifying speech, promising to go "house to house" and cleanse the city of the "cockroaches" and "rats." The prospect of a massacre spurred the international community into action. In a crucial meeting of the Arab League, Qatar, along with the UAE, led the charge in calling for the suspension of Libya's membership and urging the United Nations to impose a no-fly zone.

This diplomatic activism soon morphed into something far more radical. Qatar decided to go to war. When the UN Security Council passed Resolution 1973 authorizing military intervention to protect civilians, Qatar became the first Arab nation to commit its own military assets. In a move that stunned observers, the small Qatari Emiri Air Force deployed its French-made Mirage 2000 fighter jets to bases in Crete, from which they flew combat air patrols over Libya alongside NATO aircraft. It was an unprecedented projection of hard power, a dramatic pivot for a state that had built its influence on diplomacy and media.

Qatar's involvement, however, went far deeper than a few fighter jets. It became the primary logistical hub and financial backer for the Libyan opposition. Doha recognized the rebels' National Transitional Council as the legitimate government and reportedly spent hundreds of millions of dollars arming and training various rebel factions. Special forces operatives from Qatar were said to be on the ground, advising commanders and coordinating the delivery of weapons. This intervention was not without controversy. Critics, including some within the Libyan opposition itself, accused Qatar of bypassing the unified command structure and selectively funding Islamist-leaning militias, sowing divisions that would plague the country long after Gaddafi's fall in October 2011. For Doha, however, the Libyan campaign was a stunning success. It had helped to topple a dictator, demonstrated its military capability, and cemented its role as a decisive regional player.

The wave of uprisings soon reached Syria in March 2011, but here, the story would take a much darker and more complicated turn. When peaceful protests against the rule of Bashar al-Assad were met with lethal force, Qatar initially hesitated, wary of a conflict on the doorstep of its key ally, Turkey. But as the regime's brutality intensified, Doha's policy hardened. Along with Saudi Arabia and Turkey, Qatar became one of the most vociferous advocates for the Syrian opposition, pushing the Arab League to suspend Syria's membership and leading the call for international intervention. When a unified military response failed to materialize, Qatar, again alongside its regional partners, became a principal source of funding and arms for the rebel groups fighting to overthrow the Assad regime.

The Syrian conflict, however, proved to be a far more intractable and vicious quagmire than the one in Libya. The opposition was deeply fragmented, and the conflict quickly became a proxy war, drawing in regional and global powers. As the war descended into a grinding stalemate, increasingly extreme jihadist groups, such as Jabhat al-Nusra, an al-Qaeda affiliate, rose to prominence within the armed opposition. It was in this murky environment that Qatar's policy came under intense scrutiny. The government in Doha was accused, particularly by its regional rivals, of recklessly funneling money and weapons to hardline Islamist factions, including groups with ties to al-Qaeda. While Qatari officials vehemently denied supporting terrorist organizations, their open backing of a wide range of Islamist-aligned rebel groups created a perception of recklessness that would severely damage the country's reputation and provide potent ammunition for its detractors in the years to come.

While Qatar was championing uprisings in North Africa and the Levant, a popular protest much closer to home presented a profound challenge to its pro-democracy narrative. In February 2011, mass protests, led by the country's Shia majority, erupted in Bahrain, demanding political reform from the ruling Sunni Al Khalifa family. The demonstrations at the Pearl Roundabout in Manama mirrored those in Tahrir Square. For a moment, it seemed the Arab Spring had arrived in the Gulf.

But here, the script was flipped. For the monarchies of the Gulf, an uprising in one of their own was not a movement to be supported, but an existential threat to be crushed. In March, the GCC invoked its collective security pact. The Peninsula Shield Force, a joint military contingent, rolled across the causeway from Saudi Arabia into Bahrain to support the government's crackdown. And in that convoy were troops from the State of Qatar. The same Qatari government whose air force was preparing to protect protesters in Libya was sending its army to help suppress protesters in Bahrain. Al Jazeera, which had provided wall-to-wall coverage of the events in Cairo and Benghazi, gave the Bahraini uprising only muted and sporadic attention. This glaring contradiction laid bare the pragmatic, and some would say hypocritical, limits of Qatar's revolutionary foreign policy. When it came to the stability of the Gulf's monarchical system, solidarity trumped ideology.

The same pragmatism was evident in Yemen, where a long-simmering protest movement against President Ali Abdullah Saleh also gained momentum in 2011. Here, Qatar worked within the GCC framework to manage a transition, not to overthrow a regime. The goal was to ease the long-time ruler out of power to avoid a full-scale collapse of the state, a policy that culminated in a GCC-brokered deal for Saleh to step down in late 2011.

By 2012, Qatar's hyperactive foreign policy had made it one of the most influential, and controversial, actors in the Middle East. Its support for the Arab Spring uprisings was driven by a complex mix of factors: a genuine belief that popular movements, particularly those led by moderate Islamists like the Muslim Brotherhood, were the future; a desire to break free from the traditional dominance of Saudi Arabia; and the simple calculation that being at the center of every major regional event made the small state a big player.

But the risks were immense. The policy had created a deep and bitter ideological rift with its most powerful neighbors, Saudi Arabia and the UAE, who viewed Qatar's support for the Muslim Brotherhood as a direct threat to their own systems of rule. The bet on the Brotherhood's success was also precarious. While Qatar's ally, Mohamed Morsi, now sat in the presidential palace in Cairo, his rule was proving to be divisive and unstable.

The era of dizzying ambition and seemingly limitless possibilities was drawing to a close. The region was becoming more polarized, more violent, and less forgiving. In a move that surprised the world, Sheikh Hamad bin Khalifa Al Thani, the architect of this entire policy, decided it was time for a new generation to take the helm. On June 25, 2013, in a televised address, he announced that he was abdicating in favor of his 33-year-old son, Sheikh Tamim bin Hamad Al Thani. It was a peaceful and orderly transfer of power, unique in the modern history of the Gulf's hereditary states. It was also seen as a potential moment to reset relationships and dial down the temperature in the region.

Just eight days after the new Emir took power in Doha, the ground shifted violently under Qatar's feet. On July 3, 2013, following massive popular protests, the Egyptian military, led by General Abdel Fattah el-Sisi, overthrew President Mohamed Morsi in a coup. The move was enthusiastically welcomed and heavily financed by Saudi Arabia and the UAE. For Qatar, it was a strategic catastrophe. Its single most important ally in the new Middle East was in prison, its investment of billions of dollars had been wiped out, and its vision of a region led by like-minded Islamist governments was in ruins. The new regime in Cairo was virulently anti-Qatari, viewing Doha as the primary patron of its deposed enemy. Qatar was suddenly on the wrong side of the new regional order, its foreign policy in tatters. The deep antagonism it had fostered with its neighbors during the heady days of the Arab Spring was no longer a matter of diplomatic friction; it was now a dangerous isolation.

CHAPTER TWENTY-THREE: The 2017 Diplomatic Crisis: Blockade and Resilience

The abdication of Sheikh Hamad in 2013 and the accession of his young son, Sheikh Tamim bin Hamad Al Thani, was seen by many as a chance to reset the increasingly toxic politics of the Persian Gulf. The heady, activist foreign policy of the Arab Spring had left Qatar isolated, its bets on Islamist-led revolutions having soured, most spectacularly with the 2013 military coup in Egypt. Its powerful neighbors, Saudi Arabia and the United Arab Emirates, viewed Doha's support for the Muslim Brotherhood not as a principled stand for democracy, but as a direct threat to their own monarchical systems. The hope was that the new, younger Emir might dial down the rhetoric, rein in Al Jazeera, and bring Qatar back into the conservative fold of the Gulf Cooperation Council.

This hope proved to be short-lived. The underlying tensions were too deep, the clash of ideologies too profound. In March 2014, in a move that served as a dress rehearsal for the main event, Saudi Arabia, the UAE, and Bahrain withdrew their ambassadors from Doha. They accused Qatar of failing to abide by the terms of a hitherto secret document known as the Riyadh Agreement, signed in late 2013, in which Qatar had allegedly pledged not to interfere in the internal affairs of other GCC states, nor to support hostile media or groups like the Muslim Brotherhood. After nine months of tense mediation by the Emir of Kuwait, a supplementary agreement was reached, and the ambassadors returned. But the truce was fragile. A relentless, often vitriolic, media campaign against Qatar continued in Saudi and Emirati newspapers and television channels. The rift had been papered over, not healed.

The final rupture was preceded by an act of digital subterfuge. In the early hours of May 24, 2017, the website of the official Qatar News Agency (QNA) was hacked. A series of sensational, and entirely fabricated, statements were posted and attributed to Sheikh Tamim. The fake remarks had him praising Iran as an "Islamic power," defending Hamas and Hezbollah, and criticizing the new American administration of President Donald Trump. Qatar's Government Communications Office immediately issued a denial, stating that the agency had been hacked and that the story was false. It made no difference. The media outlets of Saudi Arabia and the UAE, seemingly prepared for the event, seized upon the fake statements and broadcast them as fact, launching a furious, coordinated media assault. The pretext, however flimsy, had been established.

On the morning of June 5, 2017, residents of Qatar woke up to a reality that was, for many, unthinkable. In a series of coordinated announcements, Saudi Arabia, the UAE, Bahrain, and Egypt declared that they were severing all diplomatic and economic ties with Doha. This was not merely a withdrawal of ambassadors. It was a comprehensive and punitive blockade designed to isolate and cripple the country. Saudi Arabia closed Qatar's only land border, through which an estimated 60 percent of its food and construction materials arrived. The four countries, dubbed the "Quartet," also closed their airspace to all Qatari-registered aircraft and barred Qatari ships from their ports. Qatari citizens living in the blockading states were given just two weeks to leave, tearing apart thousands of mixed-nationality families in the deeply interwoven societies of the Gulf.

The immediate effect in Doha was a jolt of panic. Supermarket shelves were stripped bare as residents, fearing a prolonged siege, stockpiled food and water. The country's flagship carrier, Qatar Airways, one of the pillars of its global branding strategy, was thrown into chaos. Overnight, it lost access to 18 cities and was forced to reroute its global network on longer, more expensive flight paths through Iranian and Turkish airspace. The stated justification for these drastic measures was Qatar's alleged support for terrorism and its cozy relationship with Iran—charges Doha vehemently denied.

The initial shock soon gave way to a wave of defiant nationalism. The government, tapping into its vast financial reserves, moved quickly to stabilize the economy and secure new supply lines. The initial food shortages were swiftly overcome by a massive airlift of supplies from new partners, primarily Turkey and Iran. Seaborne trade, cut off from the main regional transshipment hub of Jebel Ali in Dubai, was rerouted through the port of Salalah in Oman, which remained neutral in the dispute, and directly to Qatar's own newly expanded Hamad Port. The crisis, in a stroke of fortune, came just months after the new port had become fully operational, providing a vital lifeline that blunted the impact of the maritime siege.

About two weeks into the crisis, the blockading countries, through Kuwaiti mediators, presented Qatar with their terms for ending the standoff. It was a sweeping, non-negotiable list of 13 demands that struck at the very heart of Qatar's sovereignty and its independent foreign policy of the previous two decades. The Quartet demanded that Qatar shut down the Al Jazeera media network and its affiliates; sever all ties with organizations they designated as terrorist, specifically naming the Muslim Brotherhood, ISIS, al-Qaeda, and Hezbollah; downgrade its diplomatic relations with Iran; close the newly established Turkish military base on its soil; and hand over all designated "terrorists" and opposition figures residing in Doha. Furthermore, Qatar was to align its policies entirely with its Gulf neighbors, pay an unspecified sum in reparations, and submit to a rigorous, decade-long regime of monthly compliance audits. It was given just ten days to comply.

For the Qatari leadership, the demands were so extreme they appeared designed to be rejected. The Foreign Minister, Sheikh Mohammed bin Abdulrahman Al-Thani, branded the ultimatum an assault on the nation's sovereignty, declaring that Qatar would not be dictated to by foreign powers. The government formally rejected the demands, framing the crisis not as a dispute over policy but as a premeditated attempt to subjugate Qatar and force it to surrender its independence.

As the initial ten-day deadline passed, the crisis settled into a grinding war of attrition. The Quartet, having expected a swift capitulation, stopped short of imposing further sanctions, and the standoff became the new reality. Within Qatar, the blockade had the unintended effect of galvanizing the population. A surge of patriotic fervor swept the country, uniting citizens and long-term expatriate residents in a shared sense of defiance. The face of the Emir, Sheikh Tamim, often accompanied by the slogan "Tamim Al Majd" (Tamim the Glorious), became a ubiquitous symbol of national pride, plastered on skyscrapers, cars, and t-shirts. The crisis fostered a powerful sense of national identity forged in adversity.

The blockade also forced a radical re-engineering of the Qatari economy. With its traditional supply chains severed, the country embarked on a crash course in self-sufficiency. The most famous and symbolic example of this was in the dairy industry. Before the crisis, nearly all of Qatar's fresh milk and dairy products were imported, mostly trucked across the Saudi border. With that supply cut off overnight, a local agricultural company, Baladna, embarked on an audacious plan. In what became the largest bovine airlift in history, the company chartered dozens of cargo planes to fly in thousands of Holstein cows from Europe and the United States. Within months, massive, air-conditioned barns had been erected in the desert north of Doha, and Baladna's fresh milk was on supermarket shelves. By 2019, the country had gone from near-total dependence to complete self-sufficiency in dairy, a powerful and tangible symbol of its resilience. This drive was replicated in other sectors, with the government investing heavily to boost local production of everything from vegetables to pharmaceuticals.

Economically, the country proved remarkably resilient. The government used its massive sovereign wealth fund, the Qatar Investment Authority, to inject tens of billions of dollars into the local banking system, successfully preventing a financial crisis and stemming the outflow of capital. The annual economic growth rate, while dipping slightly in 2017, remained positive. The negative impact was largely concentrated in specific sectors like tourism, real estate, and, most notably, Qatar Airways, which reportedly lost billions due to the longer flight routes and loss of regional markets. The blockading countries also paid an economic price, with businesses in Saudi Arabia and the UAE losing a lucrative, high-margin export market.

The crisis also triggered a significant geopolitical realignment. Cut off from its immediate Arab neighbors, Qatar was forced to deepen its relationships with other powers. Turkey, which shared Qatar's sympathy for the Muslim Brotherhood, became a vital ally. Ankara fast-tracked legislation to send more troops to its military base in Qatar, a move widely seen as a deterrent against any potential military action by the blockading states. Turkish goods flooded the Qatari market, replacing those that had previously come from Saudi Arabia and the UAE.

Iran, the Quartet's primary regional adversary, also became an indispensable partner out of necessity. Iranian airspace became the main corridor for Qatar Airways flights, and Iranian ports became crucial for trade. This pushed Qatar into a closer, more pragmatic relationship with Tehran, the very thing the blockade was ostensibly designed to prevent. The diplomatic counter-offensive was relentless. Qatar engaged in a massive lobbying and public relations campaign in Western capitals, particularly in Washington D.C., to counter the narrative of the blockading states.

The role of the United States was marked by confusion in the early stages of the crisis. President Trump initially sent tweets that appeared to endorse the blockade and take credit for it, echoing the Quartet's accusations against Qatar. This stance, however, was in direct conflict with that of his own State and Defense Departments, which prized stability and valued the critical role of the Al Udeid Air Base in Qatar, the forward headquarters of U.S. Central Command. Over time, the official U.S. position shifted to one of frustrated neutrality, with Washington making repeated, unsuccessful attempts to mediate a solution.

For three and a half years, the blockade became an entrenched feature of the Middle Eastern landscape. The Gulf Cooperation Council, once a symbol of regional solidarity, was effectively shattered, its meetings becoming exercises in awkward diplomacy. The war of words, fought through competing state-sponsored media networks and armies of social media trolls, continued unabated. Qatar had not capitulated; on the contrary, the crisis seemed to have made it more resilient, more independent, and more determined to forge its own path. It had survived the initial shock, rewired its economy, and forged new alliances. The attempt to bring the maverick state to heel had not only failed, but had arguably pushed it further away from the orbit of its neighbors.

CHAPTER TWENTY-FOUR: The FIFA World Cup 2022: Triumph and Controversy

The twelve years that separated the stunning announcement in Zurich from the first whistle-blow at Al Bayt Stadium were a period of relentless, and often punishing, global scrutiny for Qatar. From the moment FIFA President Sepp Blatter pulled the small nation's name from the envelope, the 2022 World Cup became less a sporting event and more a geopolitical stress test. The project was burdened with a weight of skepticism that would have crushed a less determined host. Every aspect of the preparation, from the colossal infrastructure projects to the nation's deeply conservative social laws, was placed under an international microscope. For Qatar, the tournament was the ultimate culmination of the grand strategy set in motion by Sheikh Hamad: to use its immense wealth to force itself onto the world stage. It was a multi-hundred-billion-dollar gamble, a project of national transformation masquerading as a football tournament. The goal was not merely to host the world, but to do so in a way that was undeniably, spectacularly, and controversially Qatari.

The sheer scale of the undertaking was difficult for outsiders to comprehend. Qatar was not renovating a few stadiums and sprucing up an airport; it was building the infrastructure of a modern country at an accelerated, almost fantastical, pace. The estimated cost, a figure often cited at over $220 billion, became a headline in itself, though this number was somewhat misleading. The vast majority of that expenditure was not on the tournament directly but on the Qatar National Vision 2030, a sweeping plan for new cities, transport networks, and hotels for which the World Cup acted as an unmovable deadline and a powerful catalyst. The tournament was the deadline that forced a generation of development into a single decade.

Central to the promise made in 2010 were the stadiums, the architectural jewels designed to showcase Qatari innovation. Seven new state-of-the-art venues were constructed from scratch, and the existing Khalifa International Stadium was completely reimagined. Each was an architectural statement. The Al Bayt Stadium in Al Khor, host of the opening match, was a breathtaking structure designed to resemble a traditional Bedouin tent, or *bayt al sha'ar*. Al Janoub Stadium in Al Wakrah, designed by the late Zaha Hadid, evoked the billowing sails of the dhows that once plied the Gulf's pearling banks. The most audacious was perhaps Stadium 974, a vibrant waterfront venue constructed from 974 recycled shipping containers, a modular design that allowed it to be completely dismantled and repurposed after the tournament, a novel answer to the perennial problem of white-elephant stadiums.

Beneath the turf of these spectacular arenas lay the solution to the problem that had dogged the bid from the beginning: the climate. Fulfilling the seemingly impossible promise of the bid, all the stadiums were equipped with a revolutionary cooling system. Developed by Qatari engineers, the technology used solar power to chill water, which was then pumped through thousands of vents under the seats and larger nozzles at pitch level, creating a cool "bubble" of air within the open-roofed stadium that kept both players and spectators comfortable. Though the tournament was eventually moved to the winter, the cooling technology was still a vital component, a testament to the country's determination to overcome its natural limitations through sheer financial and technological will.

Connecting this constellation of new venues was the Doha Metro, arguably the most important single piece of infrastructure built for the tournament. In 2010, Qatar had no rail system. By 2022, it possessed one of the most advanced, and beautiful, driverless metro networks in the world. Three sleek, modern lines converged on the central hub of Msheireb, linking the airport directly to five of the eight stadiums and the major fan zones and accommodation clusters. During the tournament, it would become the circulatory system of the event, efficiently transporting hundreds of thousands of fans a day in air-conditioned comfort, a key component in delivering the promised "compact" World Cup.

While the concrete was being poured and the tracks were being laid, a storm of controversy was raging, one that would define the global narrative of the tournament long before a ball was kicked. The most damaging and persistent issue was the treatment of the vast army of migrant laborers who were the engine of this construction miracle. Coming primarily from South Asia and Africa, these workers toiled under the restrictive *kafala* sponsorship system, which tied a worker's legal status directly to their employer, a system critics likened to modern-day indentured servitude. Reports from human rights organizations and international media painted a grim picture of low wages, squalid living conditions, and hazardous worksites.

The issue of worker deaths became the most explosive point of contention. In February 2021, an investigation by *The Guardian* newspaper published a shocking figure, claiming that more than 6,500 migrant workers from India, Pakistan, Nepal, Bangladesh, and Sri Lanka had died in Qatar since it won the World Cup bid in 2010. This number, though not differentiating between World Cup-related projects and other deaths, became a global rallying cry for critics of the tournament. Qatari officials vehemently disputed the figure, arguing that it was a misleading and sensationalized total that failed to reflect the size of the migrant population and the actual number of workplace accidents. The official records from the Supreme Committee for Delivery & Legacy, the body overseeing tournament construction, listed three work-related fatalities and 37 non-work-related deaths on stadium projects. The vast disparity between these figures fueled a bitter and emotional debate that cast a long shadow over the event.

Under the glare of this intense international pressure, Qatar was forced to act. In what was perhaps the most significant, and unlikeliest, legacy of the tournament, the government undertook a series of sweeping labor reforms, often in direct partnership with the International Labour Organization (ILO), a UN agency. In 2017, Qatar signed an agreement with the ILO to overhaul its labor laws. Over the next few years, the most egregious elements of the *kafala* system were dismantled. The requirement for an exit permit, which had prevented workers from leaving the country without their employer's permission, was abolished. In 2020, in a landmark move for the region, Qatar introduced a non-discriminatory minimum wage and made it easier for workers to change jobs. While human rights groups acknowledged the reforms were significant, they continued to highlight persistent issues with implementation and wage theft, arguing that the changes, while welcome, had come too late for many.

As the tournament drew closer, the focus of the controversy shifted to social issues. Concerns were repeatedly raised about the safety and welcome that would be extended to LGBTQ+ fans in a country where homosexual acts are illegal. FIFA and Qatari officials insisted that "all were welcome," but the messaging was often mixed and confusing. One Qatari official designated as a World Cup ambassador was widely condemned for calling homosexuality "damage in the mind" in a German television interview just weeks before the tournament. The issue came to a head over the "OneLove" armbands that the captains of several European teams, including England, Germany, and the Netherlands, planned to wear to promote diversity and inclusion. In a last-minute standoff, FIFA threatened the players with sporting sanctions, including yellow cards, if they wore the unapproved armbands. The teams backed down, but the German team registered its protest in a team photo before their opening match against Japan, the players covering their mouths to signify they had been silenced.

Another flashpoint revolved around the sale of alcohol. While not a dry country, the public consumption of alcohol in Qatar is strictly limited to licensed hotels and restaurants. For months, organizers had worked on a compromise, planning to allow the sale of Budweiser, a major FIFA sponsor, in designated areas around the stadiums. Then, just two days before the opening match, in an abrupt reversal, the decision was made to ban all alcohol sales at the eight stadium sites. The move was seen by many as a reassertion of conservative local values over the expectations of international fans and a major embarrassment for FIFA.

Finally, on November 20, 2022, after twelve years of debate, construction, and controversy, the tournament began. The opening ceremony at the spectacular Al Bayt Stadium was a carefully choreographed message of global unity and Arab pride. In a notable break with tradition, the ceremony was not just a celebration of the host nation, but a wider appeal to multiculturalism, famously featuring the American actor Morgan Freeman in conversation with a young Qatari disabled activist and YouTuber, Ghanim Al-Muftah.

Once the football began, however, the narrative started to shift. The tournament on the pitch was, by almost universal consensus, a spectacular success. The compact nature of the event, once a point of skepticism, proved to be a masterstroke. Fans could, and often did, attend two or even three matches in a single day, traveling seamlessly between venues on the new metro. The atmosphere in the city, while different from the more raucous, alcohol-fueled fan cultures of previous World Cups, was festive and remarkably safe. The Souq Waqif, Doha's traditional market, became the vibrant, multicultural heart of the tournament, a nightly celebration of the thirty-two competing nations.

The football itself was consistently thrilling, filled with dramatic upsets that captured the imagination of the world. In the first week, Saudi Arabia stunned Lionel Messi's Argentina in one of the biggest shocks in the tournament's history. Japan pulled off improbable victories against the European powerhouses of Germany and Spain. But the fairytale story of the tournament belonged to Morocco. The "Atlas Lions," roared on by passionate support from across the Arab world, defied all expectations, defeating Belgium, Spain, and Portugal on a historic run to the semi-finals. They became the first African and first Arab nation ever to reach the final four of a World Cup, a moment of immense pride that resonated far beyond the borders of Qatar.

The final, held on December 18, Qatar's National Day, was the perfect climax to a remarkable tournament. The magnificent, golden-hued Lusail Stadium played host to what many immediately hailed as the greatest World Cup final of all time. It was a titanic struggle between the reigning champions, France, led by the electrifying Kylian Mbappé, and Argentina, led by the iconic Lionel Messi in what was to be his last World Cup match. The game was a rollercoaster of emotion, with Argentina dominating for eighty minutes before a quick-fire brace from Mbappé forced extra time. Messi scored again, only for Mbappé to complete his hat-trick from the penalty spot in the dying moments. The match, tied 3-3, went to a penalty shootout, where Argentina finally prevailed, securing a third world title and providing the crowning moment of Messi's legendary career.

The trophy presentation provided one final, iconic image that perfectly encapsulated the tournament's blend of triumph and cultural contention. As Lionel Messi prepared to lift the trophy, Qatar's Emir, Sheikh Tamim bin Hamad Al Thani, draped a *bisht*—a traditional, semi-transparent black cloak edged with gold, worn by men in the Arab world on formal occasions as a sign of respect and honor—over the Argentine captain's shoulders. For many in the Arab world, it was a beautiful and fitting gesture, a mark of high esteem that welcomed a global icon into their culture. For many Western commentators, however, it was a bizarre and unwelcome intrusion, a move that covered up the famous blue-and-white stripes of the Argentine shirt and marred a sacred footballing moment with a piece of local regalia. This single, simple act crystallized the entire twelve-year saga: a small nation had successfully hosted the world, but it had insisted on doing so on its own terms, leaving a legacy as complex and debated as the decision to award it the tournament in the first place.

CHAPTER TWENTY-FIVE: Qatar in the 21st Century: Challenges and Future Prospects

When the last of the football fans departed from Hamad International Airport in late December 2022, a strange quiet descended upon Qatar. For twelve frantic years, the country had been a giant construction site with a singular, unmovable deadline. The FIFA World Cup had acted as a national organizing principle, a catalyst that compressed a generation of development into a decade. Now, the party was over. The stadiums stood silent, the new metro ran with quiet efficiency, and the country woke up to the first day of the rest of its life. The question that had long been deferred was now front and center: What comes next? Having spent hundreds of billions of dollars to build the stage and host the world, Qatar faced the challenge of defining its purpose in a post-tournament era, navigating the treacherous currents of regional politics and a global energy transition that threatened the very foundation of its prosperity.

The first, and most crucial, step in securing this future had actually been taken nearly two years before the tournament began. On January 5, 2021, at a GCC summit held in the historic Saudi city of Al-Ula, the leaders of the Gulf states and Egypt signed a "solidarity and stability" agreement. The Al-Ula Declaration formally brought the painful, three-and-a-half-year blockade of Qatar to an end. Following months of quiet diplomacy, spearheaded by Kuwait and the final push by the outgoing Trump administration, Saudi Arabia, the UAE, Bahrain, and Egypt agreed to restore full diplomatic ties and reopen their land, sea, and air borders with Qatar. The Emir, Sheikh Tamim bin Hamad Al Thani, flew to the summit, where he was greeted on the tarmac with a warm embrace from Saudi Crown Prince Mohammed bin Salman, a powerful piece of political theater that signaled a formal end to the hostilities. The original 13 demands, which Qatar had decried as an assault on its sovereignty, were quietly dropped in favor of a general commitment to joint security and regional stability.

The reconciliation was more a pragmatic truce than a warm reunion. Relations with Saudi Arabia improved quickly, driven by a mutual desire to de-escalate regional tensions and focus on their ambitious domestic economic agendas. The reopening of the land border was a huge practical and symbolic relief for Qatar. Ties with the UAE and Bahrain, however, took longer to thaw, their deep ideological opposition to Qatar's foreign policy and its support for Islamist movements not easily erased by a single declaration. Nevertheless, the end of the blockade was a significant victory for Qatar. It had not only survived the intense pressure campaign but had arguably emerged more resilient and economically independent. The crisis had forced it to diversify its trade routes, boost local production, and deepen alliances with powers like Turkey. It had refused to capitulate, and its neighbors had ultimately decided that a fractured Gulf was a greater threat to their own stability than an independent-minded Qatar.

With the neighborhood relatively calm, Qatar turned its attention to the engine room of its entire national project: the North Field. While the world grappled with the challenges of climate change and the transition to renewable energy, Qatar made a colossal bet in the opposite direction, doubling down on its status as the world's indispensable supplier of liquefied natural gas. Even before the World Cup, the state-owned behemoth QatarEnergy had sanctioned a massive expansion project, lifting a self-imposed 12-year moratorium on new developments. The plan was breathtaking in its scale. The first phase, the North Field East (NFE) project, aims to construct four new LNG "trains," boosting Qatar's annual production capacity from 77 million tonnes to 110 million tonnes by 2025. This was swiftly followed by a second phase, the North Field South (NFS), which would add two more trains, taking capacity to 126 million tonnes per annum by 2027.

Then, in a surprise announcement in February 2024, after new geological surveys revealed the field was even larger than previously thought, a third expansion was unveiled. The "North

Field West" project would add another 16 million tonnes of capacity, bringing the total target to an astounding 142 million tonnes per annum before the end of the decade. This represented an 85 percent increase in production from pre-expansion levels. The strategy was clear: to leverage Qatar's position as one of the world's lowest-cost producers to lock in market share for decades to come. As Western nations sought to wean themselves off Russian gas following the 2022 invasion of Ukraine, Qatar became the go-to partner for long-term energy security, signing massive, multi-decade supply deals with European and Asian customers. The gas revolution that began in the 1990s was entering its second, even more powerful, act. This expansion was the financial bedrock that would underwrite every other aspect of the Qatar National Vision 2030.

This immense financial firepower continued to fuel Qatar's hyperactive diplomacy. The country solidified its reputation as the region's indispensable mediator, the address that everyone called when a difficult conversation was needed. This role was thrown into sharp relief in August 2021 with the chaotic collapse of the Western-backed government in Afghanistan. As the Taliban swept into Kabul, Qatar, which had hosted the U.S.-Taliban peace talks for years, became the central hub for the frantic international evacuation effort. Roughly half of all people airlifted from the country transited through Qatar. After the U.S. embassy in Kabul was shuttered, Qatar agreed to formally represent American interests in Afghanistan, its diplomats becoming the key go-between for Washington and the new Taliban government.

This role as a trusted interlocutor for all sides was tested as never before by the outbreak of war between Israel and Hamas in October 2023. Qatar, which hosts Hamas's political office in Doha at the request of the United States, was immediately thrust into the center of the frantic efforts to de-escalate the conflict and secure the release of hostages. Working alongside the U.S. and Egypt, Qatari negotiators shuttled between the warring parties, their unique access to the Hamas leadership making them a critical, if controversial, channel of communication. These efforts led to a seven-day truce in November 2023 that saw the release of over

100 hostages in exchange for Palestinian prisoners. The mediation was a high-wire act that brought both international praise and intense criticism, particularly from some quarters in the U.S. and Israel who questioned Qatar's ties to the group. For Doha, however, it was a practical application of its long-standing foreign policy doctrine: maintaining open lines of communication with all actors, no matter how difficult, is essential for resolving conflict.

Domestically, the end of the World Cup boom presented a new set of challenges. The construction frenzy, which had driven economic growth for a decade, inevitably slowed, raising concerns about the future utilization of the vast infrastructure that had been built. The government's focus shifted toward the less glamorous but crucial work of implementing the Third National Development Strategy, the next five-year plan designed to make the goals of the QNV 2030 a reality. The strategy prioritizes boosting the private sector, attracting foreign investment into non-energy fields like logistics and technology, and making tourism a sustainable industry rather than a one-off event. Plans were put in place to repurpose the World Cup stadiums; some would have their capacities reduced to serve local football clubs, while others were slated for transformation into mixed-use community hubs with schools, medical clinics, and commercial spaces.

The intense spotlight of the World Cup also left a complex legacy on the social front, particularly concerning labor rights. The sweeping reforms undertaken in the years leading up to the tournament—including the effective dismantling of the kafala system and the introduction of a minimum wage—were significant and lasting. Post-2022, the government has continued to work with the International Labour Organization to address persistent gaps in enforcement, launching new platforms to help workers switch jobs and resolve disputes. While critics maintain that the transformation is incomplete, the reforms represent a fundamental shift in the landscape of migrant labor in the Gulf, a process undeniably accelerated by the pressures of hosting the tournament.

Looking toward 2030 and beyond, Qatar faces a series of profound, long-term challenges. The existential threat of climate change looms large for a low-lying desert peninsula. The global energy transition, however slow, will eventually erode the demand for its primary export, making the race to diversify the economy a matter of national survival. The demographic imbalance, with a small citizen population in a sea of expatriate workers, remains a source of ongoing social and cultural tension. The country continues to navigate a complex and often volatile regional security environment, balancing its vital security partnership with the United States, which operates the Al Udeid Air Base, against the need for a pragmatic, working relationship with its powerful neighbor, Iran.

Yet, the nation that looks to this uncertain future is vastly different from the one that existed at the turn of the century. It is wealthier, more resilient, and more deeply integrated into the global system than ever before. It has weathered a political and economic siege, hosted the world's biggest sporting event against all odds, and established itself as a crucial diplomatic and energy hub. The journey from a sparsely populated strip of desert known only for its pearls to a global player at the center of international finance, media, and diplomacy has been one of the most rapid and improbable national transformations in modern history. The challenges remain immense, but the quiet confidence of a nation that has consistently defied expectations is now its most valuable, and perhaps most enduring, asset.

AFTERWORD

To conclude a history of Qatar is, in many ways, an artificial act. The story does not feel finished; it feels as though it is still in its breathless, high-octane introductory chapters. To stand on the Doha Corniche today, looking out at the forest of skyscrapers that claw at the sky, is to be confronted with a sense of profound temporal dissonance. The physical reality of the place—its gleaming metro, its architectural marvels, its man-made islands—seems to have no logical connection to the historical reality that this book has chronicled. Less than a century ago, this same shoreline was a humble collection of low-slung coral-and-mud houses, its waters crowded not with luxury yachts but with the wooden dhows of the pearling fleet. The sheer velocity of the transformation is difficult to process. It is a history that has unfolded not in centuries, but in decades, a story lived in fast-forward.

In writing this book, I have been repeatedly struck by this theme of improbable change. The narrative of Qatar is a cascade of moments where a different turn, a less audacious decision, would have resulted in an utterly different reality. What if Sheikh Jassim had not risked everything in the sands of Al Wajbah? What if Sheikh Abdullah had failed to secure the protection of the British? What if, in the depths of the post-pearling depression, the geologists at Dukhan had come up empty? And perhaps most consequentially, what if Sheikh Khalifa's government in the 1980s had listened to the cautious advice of international experts and deemed the North Field too risky, too expensive, too technologically challenging to develop?

The history of this peninsula is a testament to the power of strategic gambling. It is the story of a leadership that, time and again, understood that for a state of its size, the greatest risk was to do nothing, to be passive. From Sheikh Jassim playing the Ottomans against the British to Sheikh Hamad using Al Jazeera and the Al Udeid airbase as two sides of the same strategic coin, the recurring theme is one of proactive, often perilous, engagement with the world. Qatar's history is a masterclass in how a small state can leverage its few assets—be they strategic location, a single commodity, or immense capital—to create an outsized influence. It has never had the luxury of relying on demographic weight or military might. Its survival has depended on being cleverer, quicker, and more audacious than its larger neighbors.

This audacity, of course, has come with immense contradictions, and to write this history is to constantly navigate these paradoxes. How does one reconcile a state that hosts the forward headquarters of U.S. Central Command with one that maintains an open dialogue with the Taliban and Hamas? How does a nation that champions a free-wheeling and critical Arab media in the form of Al Jazeera maintain its own internal system of absolute monarchy and limited freedom of expression? How does a society that projects an image of hyper-modernity through its architecture and global investments grapple with the deeply conservative social and religious values that anchor its identity?

There are no simple answers to these questions. To search for a single, consistent ideology in Qatar's story is a futile exercise. What one finds instead is a powerful and persistent pragmatism, a foreign and domestic policy that is less about ideology and more about a hard-nosed calculation of national survival and relevance. Qatar has made itself a hub for all conversations, a place where sworn enemies can meet, a geopolitical Switzerland with a much more activist streak. This has frequently infuriated its allies and neighbors, who crave the certainty of fixed alliances and clear ideological lines. But for Qatar, this ambiguity is not a flaw in the system; it is the system. It is what makes the country useful, and therefore, secure.

This history is also, inescapably, a story about wealth on a scale that defies easy comprehension. The sheer financial power unlocked by liquefied natural gas has enabled a form of statecraft that is unique. It is a power that has allowed Qatar to build a world-class airline, to endow elite universities, to buy iconic global assets, to fund rebel movements, and to host the most expensive FIFA World Cup in history. But as this narrative has shown, the story of Qatar is not merely the story of its money. It is the story of how that money has been deliberately and strategically deployed to achieve non-financial ends: security, influence, and prestige.

Yet, in tracing this grand narrative of state-building and global ambition, it is the human story that often leaves the most lasting impression. It is the story of the pearl diver, the *ghais*, whose perilous labor sustained the peninsula for centuries, only to see his entire world vanish in the face of a cultured pearl from Japan. It is the story of the migrant worker from Nepal or the Philippines who left his family to build the gleaming stadiums and towers, his sweat and sacrifice the invisible foundation of the modern state. And it is the story of the Qatari citizen, a member of a tiny minority in their own country, who is navigating the bewildering transition from a traditional, close-knit society to a globalized, multicultural metropolis in the space of their own lifetime. The social contract that has been forged—a cradle-to-grave welfare state in exchange for political allegiance—is a powerful one, but the long-term questions of national identity and civic participation remain profound and unresolved.

As we look to the future, the lessons of this history offer a guide. Qatar has proven itself to be a nation of remarkable resilience. It has survived the collapse of its founding industry, the chaos of regional wars on its doorstep, and a punishing three-and-a-half-year blockade designed to break its will. This history of overcoming existential challenges suggests a deep well of adaptability. Yet, the challenges of the 21st century—the global transition away from hydrocarbons, the existential threat of climate change to a low-lying desert state, the social pressures of its unique demographics—are of a different magnitude.

The journey from the sparse encampments of the Neolithic age to the floodlit spectacle of the World Cup final is, by any measure, one of humanity's more improbable stories. It serves as a powerful reminder that history is not a preordained path, but a series of choices. The Qatar of today was not inevitable. It was built, decision by audacious decision, gamble by perilous gamble. The story is far from over. The quiet that descended after the World Cup was the silence of a nation catching its breath before plunging into the next, uncertain chapter of its remarkable history.

Printed in Dunstable, United Kingdom